Gypsies and Flamenco

Gypsies and Flamenco
The emergence of the art of flamenco in Andalusia

Bernard Leblon
translated by Sinéad ní Shuinéar

GYPSY RESEARCH CENTRE

UNIVERSITY OF HERTFORDSHIRE PRESS

The *Interface Collection* is co-ordinated and developed by the Gypsy Research Centre
at the Université René Descartes in Paris.

The views expressed in this work are the author's and do not necessarily reflect those of the
Publisher, nor of the Gypsy Research Centre of the
Université René Descartes or its research groups
(historians, linguists, education specialists and others).

The Director of the *Interface Collection* is Jean-Pierre Liégeois.

This new edition published in Great Britain in 2003 by
University of Hertfordshire Press
Learning and Information Services
University of Hertfordshire
College Lane
Hatfield
Hertfordshire AL10 9AB

ISBN 1-902806-05-0 paperback

British Library Cataloguing in Publication Data
A catalogue record for this book is available from the British Library

Design by Geoff Green, Cambridge CB4 5RA
Cover design by John Robertshaw, Harpenden AL5 2TB
Printed in Great Britain by Antony Rowe Ltd., Chippenham SN14 6LH

About the Author

Bernard Leblon's first contacts with the Gypsy world and with flamenco, in Seville in the 1950s, had a profound influence on his life. Since the 1960s he has been engaged in research into the history of the Gypsies of Spain, culminating, in 1980, in a doctoral thesis on the subject. He set up a specialised research centre at the University of Perpignan, where he was professor of Hispanic studies until his retirement in 1994.

A participant in flamenco congresses since 1982, and a member of the Andalusian Flamenco Foundation since its inception in 1987, he was a member of the board of directors of the Gypsy Research Centre of the Université René Descartes and of its associated Research Group on European Gypsy History.

M. Leblon's first work on flamenco, *Musiques tsiganes et Flamenco* (Gypsy Music Styles and Flamenco), co-published by *Etudes Tsiganes** and Harmattan, 1990, was awarded the 1988 Andalusian Flamenco Foundation prize.

Contents

Picture credits

pii, p16, p52, pp58–9 and *p74–5* Photographs by Jean Loustalot

pxii Engraving by Lucas of Leiden, sixteenth century. F. Lugt Collection, Netherlands Institute, Paris

p2 Gaasbeck Museum, Belgium. Photograph courtesy of Mme Fabri, Brussels

p3 From *Balint Sarosi* (Gypsy Music), Cozvina Press, Budapest, 1970

p4 Drawing by Valério in *Musée Universel*, 1876

p7, p9, p68 and *pp82–3* Photographs by Michel Dieuzaide

p11 Drawing by Louis Leloir, nineteenth century

p12 Engraving by A. Rouargue

p25 Archivo Histórico Nacional, Consejo de Castilla, 1695, folio 211

pp26–7 Photograph by Jan Kuba

p32 Drawing by A. Rouargue in *Magasin Pittoresque*, 1854

p35 Photograph by Marc Gourmelon

p40 Maps drawn up by the Department of Geography at the University of Toulouse

p41 Archivo General de Simancas, Gracia y Justicia, Leg. 1005

p44 Map drawn up by the Department of Geography at the University of Toulouse

p48 Engraving by Gustave Doré for *Le Voyage en Espagne* by Théophile Gauthier

p54 Lithograph by A. Mouilleron, Imprimerie Bertauts, Paris

p63 Lithograph by Villain, Bibliothèque Nationale de Paris (F. de Vaux de Foletier Collection)

Part One

Gypsy bagpipe-player in the Netherlands

Introduction

H istorically, Flamenco studies and research on the Gitanos – the
Gypsies of Spain – have overlapped very little. As work progresses
in these fields – and it must be noted that both are very recent developments, dating only from the 1960s – research has become increasingly
specialised, making any attempt at synthesis more and more difficult.
There is a danger of concentrating on individual phenomena in isolation
from the broader picture. Thus the wrongheaded theories frequently pro-
pounded with regard to the relationship between Gypsies and music have
been facilitated by their authors' ignorance of the situation beyond the
borders of their own country, or even of their own particular region of it.
There is even a fairly entrenched tendency among Andalusians to consider 'their' Gypsies – the *Betica** Gypsies, as some call them – as
having nothing whatever in common with Gypsies elsewhere, an assump-
tion which has led some imaginative authors to posit an entirely separate
origin and history for them. Clearly, such mistakes can only be remedied
through international research co-operation.

Long before such collaboration began, though, I had the good fortune
to benefit from a very particular set of circumstances. I first visited
Andalusia in the 1950s, when I was initiated into flamenco music
through my guitar-playing. A little later, in the early 1960s, my perspec-
tives on Gypsy music were broadened through meetings organised by
Etudes Tsiganes and by unexpectedly meeting André Hajdu, a Hungarian
musicologist in exile in Paris. The ensuing years, to 1979, were spent
researching a doctorate thesis on Gitano history, and it wasn't until I had
completed it that I was able to get back into flamenco circles. This in turn
launched me into new research.

The point of this biographical detail is to explain how it has been possible for me to link up fields which up to now have been entirely separate: Gitano history and flamenco on the one hand, and on the other a comparative study of the music of Andalusian Gypsies and of the Gypsies of Central Europe. If not for these particular circumstances, I would have been unable to perceive the links which eventually proved indispensable in discovering the origins of flamenco. The question is far from being resolved, but at this point we *have* progressed beyond mere speculation. On the contrary, the following pages present a set of data which are precise and, though sometimes subtle, very concrete.

Chapter 1 retraces the crucial stages of the journey of professional Gypsy musicians from India to Spain, and aims primarily at highlighting those shared characteristics which enable us to define a 'family likeness' running through the various styles of Gypsy music.

Chapter 2 deals with the forced settlement of the Gypsy population of Spain between the time of the Catholic Monarchs* and the end of the eighteenth century. This dark period forms an essential backdrop to understanding the conditions of acculturation within which the new art-form known as *flamenco* sprang into being.

Chapter 3 concentrates on a number of families established for the past three or four centuries in a very precise region of Lower Andalusia in what have at times been rather unique conditions, and who have played a decisive role in the development of flamenco music.

The fourth chapter attempts to summarise and critique existing hypotheses on the origins of flamenco, and to draw some conclusions without straying beyond the facts of which we can be certain.

CHAPTER ONE

The Gypsies, professional musicians

N orth-west India, the Gypsies' place of origin, appears to have played an important role in the development of Oriental music. Several Iranian texts relate a rather curious legend in connection with this subject. The earliest of these texts is a history of the kings of Persia written by the Arab historian Hamza of Ispahan (Hamza Ibn Hasan-al-Isfalani) in the mid-tenth century, the latest is *The Book of Kings (Shahnameh)* by the Persian poet Firdausi, dating from the early eleventh century.

According to these authors, the Sassanid king Bahram V, who reigned in Persia in the early fifth century (420–438), was moved to pity by the realisation that the poorest of his subjects could not celebrate festivities because musicians' fees were beyond their reach. He wrote to his brother-in-law, King Shankal of Kannauj (in northern India), who, so the story goes, responded by sending him musicians from his kingdom (12,000 of them, according to Hamza, who calls them *Zott*; a mere 10,000 according to Firdausi's poem, where they are called *Luri*). Once they had arrived, Bahram gave them donkeys, cattle and seed grain, so that they could cultivate the earth. All he demanded in return was that they play music free of charge for the poor. A year later they returned to him, pale and famished. They had contented themselves with playing music, and had eaten their grain and beef without taking the trouble to sow or to labour. Greatly annoyed, Bahram advised them to string their lutes with silk, take their donkeys and begone, travelling the world and making their living with their music. Of course such anecdotal evidence recalls the Gypsies, particularly as the term *Zott* is among those used by the Arabs to designate them.

'The Little Dancing Girl', detail of a tapestry from Tournai

From East to West

The Gypsies certainly spent a considerable period in Iran, as indicated by the numerous Persian loan-words in their language, Romani. They exercised their talents as professional musicians in that country, and they contributed to the diffusion of Oriental musical instruments and styles both throughout the Arab world and the West. As regards Arab countries, we know that in Egypt – where musical styles (*maqamat*) are generally of Iranian origin – Gypsy musicians continue to play a very important role, as do *ghawazi* or gypsy dancing-girls. Further west, a great deal can be learned through tracing the diffusion of instruments, such as the *tambura*, a Persian lute to be found as far afield as Serbia; the *santur*, a sort of dulcimer, also Persian, which becomes the *sandouri* in Greece and the *cymbalom* (*czimbalom*) in Hungary; and the *nay*, whose name means 'reed' in Iran and designates the Pan pipes in Romania and the straight flute found throughout the Muslim world.

The first instruments Western chroniclers noted as being played by Gypsies were lutes, mentioned in Dubrovnik on the Dalmatian coast, and

Hungarian Gypsy Musicians

Gypsy musicians

in Hungary, both in the fifteenth century. In the latter country the *czimbalom*, mentioned above, was already being cited as a Gypsy specialty. In France, a little later, the Gypsies were considered expert harpists, and indeed for a time appear to have enjoyed a monopoly of that instrument.

Turkey and Greece

In many Muslim countries certain religious prejudices against music left the field wide open to Gypsy practitioners, who sometimes had it entirely to themselves. This is particularly the case among the Kurds of Turkey, where the drums (*davul*), oboe (*zurna*) and triangular violin (*kemançe*) are reserved exclusively for Gypsies. This is why in several regions of Europe, such as Greece, the words *Gypsy* and *musician* are synonymous even today. Nick Davanellos, a Greek musicologist, describes how Gypsies have been going from village to village to celebrate *panegiri* (votive festivals in honour of the local patron saint) for a very long time. Formerly they frequently travelled in pairs, one playing the *pipiza*, a sort of whistle made from a small reed, the other a flat drum called a *daouli* (the Turkish *davul*). The *pipiza* was introduced to Greece between the thirteenth and sixteenth centuries by Gypsy musicians coming in from Asia. These also brought in the Arab lute (*'ud*), the *sandouri*, and the *defi* – a drum along the lines of those known as *def* or *duff* in Asia. Dr Davanellos continues:

> The Rom did not only play hymns on patron saints' days; they played at weddings, christenings, and in the taverns at night. They went from house to house playing Christmas carols and Easter psalms. They were the only musicians present at every festival, every celebration. They brought life, joy and happiness to everyone taking part.

This is why Greek music is tinged with a Gypsy flavour, at once so remarkable and so indefinable. Gypsies have been professional travelling musicians just about everywhere, particularly in Central Europe, whence the evident 'Gypsification' of Romanian, Hungarian, Czech, Slovak, Russian and even Ashkenazi Jewish music.

Once we understand that, from the sixteenth century, Gypsies were already playing 'in the Turkish manner' for the pashas occupying Hungary, and 'in the Hungarian manner' for the Magyar princes under occupation, we can form some idea of the incredible musical synthesis achieved by these musicians within the musical cultures of a large part of Europe and the Mediterranean world. While interpreting local music to suit the tastes of their clients, they have always done so in their own way, permeating folk tunes and popular airs with their own musical traditions and, perhaps to an even greater degree, with their own way of living, feeling, and expressing music. In some cases, new musical styles were born out of this extraordinary encounter of East and West through Gypsy intermediaries.

Hungarian 'Gypsy' music falls into this category, as do some types of Greek music, and, of course, flamenco, the subject of this volume.

Hungary

A situation exists in Hungary which is somewhat comparable to that in Andalusia. Leaving aside the 'Wallachians' or *Vlax* for the time being, who will serve as reference points later on, let us consider the music played professionally by Gypsies of the so-called 'Hungarian' or *Romungro**, group. The success of these Gypsy musicians in the sixteenth century continued to grow over the following centuries, and the great Hungarian families kept whole orchestras of them, generally comprising violins, a double bass, sometimes a few bagpipes and/or clarinets, and, of course, the *czimbalom*. Ensembles of this type were also to be found playing at the dances of humbler folk and, more surprisingly, accompanying recruiting sergeants as they made their rounds from village to village. Gypsy musicians, dressed for the occasion in dapper Hussars' uniforms, were set up in a corner of the village square, and drink was plied on local youths, the music and wine together beguiling them into signing up. This was how *verbunkos* music, the so-called recruiting-sergeants' dance, was born; towards 1835 it was to develop into the *csardas*, a name drawn from *csárda*, the tavern of the *puszta*. This music has an Oriental structure, with a fairly slow prelude known as a *lassu*, *lassan*, or *keserrgö* (lament) and a fast and furious finale called a *friss* or *friska*. Its exhilarating effects have become legendary. In a letter dated 1854, Prosper Mérimée recorded:

> It starts with something very lugubrious and finishes with a mad gaiety that wins over the listener, who stamps his feet, smashes glasses and dances on the tables.

It should be noted that Gypsies were not only interpreters but generally also composers of the musical styles known as *verbunkos* and *csardas*. The most celebrated of these was Janos Bihari, who in 1808 composed the *Krönungs-Nota* (also known as the *Bihari-Nota*) for the coronation of the Empress Maria Louisa, and who also collaborated in the composition of the famous *Rakóczi March*, later to become the Hungarian national anthem. In an era when conventional wisdom in Hungary as in Spain denies any creative input from Gypsies, it is important to emphasise these details, and to recall that Bihari exerted a very strong influence over his

contemporaries such as Ferenc Erkel, Mihaly Mosonyi and Franz Liszt.

These instrumental styles, some Gypsy, some Hungarian, in fact embrace diverse influences, in particular Turkish ones – notably in the manner of playing the violin – and, of course, a very Gypsy genius for the aptly timed switch from languid melancholy to unbridled frenzy. Apart from these specialties of *Romungro* professionals, Hungary has other, more folkloric music styles, which are more authentically Hungarian. Yet here too the role of travelling musicians had a decisive impact and some of these styles are interpreted in the Gypsy manner to this day. Gypsy influence is also noticeable in popular song, which appeared around 1840 as a sort of mélange of the various tendencies mentioned above. We shall return to this subject.

Gypsy 'flavour' and the *duende**

It is impossible to list all the musical styles played by Gypsy professionals, even if we were to limit ourselves to Europe. They display important differences in accordance with the habits and preferences imposed by indigenous musical cultures, yet all demonstrate a singular congruence and even a certain 'family resemblance', attesting to the *Gypsy* temperament of the musicians involved. What exactly is this famous temperament, this strange Gypsy 'flavour', immediately recognisable regardless of instrument or style? This is undoubtedly the hardest thing to define, since it can take such varied forms. In instrumental music it is often a diabolical virtuosity that takes your breath away, for it is never mechanical, but always animated by a sort of Dionysian trance. In slow movements, it is an exaggerated languor, the bitterest and sweetest melancholy, nostalgia at its tenderest and most cruel. In rapid passages it is a fervour, an unchaining of the senses, a paroxysm uniting a singer in Moscow and a dancer in Seville, Ankara musicians and Jerez *buleaeros** in the same raging flame.

Jarko Jovanovic, the great Yugoslavian Gypsy musician who died in Paris in 1986, defined one of the styles he interpreted as follows:

> Fevered, soaring, tempestuous, extravagant, erotic, fragile, subtle, bitter and full of the sufferings of love … It strikes straight at the emotions.

The strings may be squeaky and worn, the voice cracked and hoarse – what counts here is not the pure and polished sound imposed by the anxious academicism of our conservatories, but outrageous expressivity, a

sound too human to be heard without a total upheaval of one's being, a heartrending cry that rips through the guts and immerses the listener in the sacred ecstasy of the *duende**. In the argot of flamenco, one does not say that a voice is beautiful, but rather that it 'hurts'; it is not meant to *please* the listener, but to wound him like a dagger brandished in passion.

Federico García Lorca noted that the *duende* (which he defined, using an expression borrowed from Goethe, as '*a mysterious power that every-one feels and no philosopher can explain*') enables the poorest material, the singer with no breath and no voice, the oldest, fattest dancer, to tri-umph. The best Gypsy music is by no means that displaying the greatest brilliance or virtuosity, but rather that which comes closest to an ideal which can be summarised as: '*maximum efficiency through minimum means*'. Just as the best *coplas* flamencas* can express the entire gamut of human emotion in two or three sibylline lines, the *duende* verges on the miraculous, like a dance on a tightrope stretched to breaking point. It can never be achieved without risk, it is never repeated and cannot be taught. The Gypsies say it's in the blood; Lorca too:

> The duende is therefore a power, not a way of behaving; a struggle, not an idea. I have heard an old master guitarist say, 'The duende is not in the throat; the duende comes from within, from the very soles of the feet.' That is to say, it is not a question of a faculty but of a truly living style, of a very old culture, of creation in action.

Spain

In Spain as elsewhere, the Gypsies quickly gained a reputation as profes-sional musicians, and from the late sixteenth century onwards were regu-lar participants in popular festivities connected with Corpus Christi in many Spanish cities, such as Toledo, where their presence was noted in 1593, 1596 and 1604, and Segovia, where their participation was recorded in 1613, 1624, and 1628. In Grenada, this participation dates from 1607, when the Moors (Arabs recently converted to Christianity) were excluded from the festival and, two years later, expelled from the country. Writing in the same period, Cervantes gives us a description, in *La Gitanilla* (The Little Gypsy Girl), of the travels of the heroine and her troupe from village to village to enliven votive festivals by dancing in the streets. These Gypsy performances enjoyed such success that they were quickly imitated on theatre stages, and prompted a law signed by Philip IV in 1633 which sought to ban them.

The 'Gypsy' repertoire

Dance with guitar and tambourine

The professional repertoire of the Gypsies of Spain during the Golden Age is well known. Some songs come down from the most authentically Spanish tradition, among them the *romances** – ancient narrative ballads with a fairytale or legendary content, many versions of which have been preserved thanks to their oral transmission in certain Gitano families – and the *seguidillas**, which are generally danced to. Of very ancient origin, these are a living component of Spanish folklore to the present day, having attained enormous popularity under the name of *Sevillenas*.

Over the years, the remainder of the repertoire has comprised the popular dances that come and go with changing fashions, such as the *polvico*, the *zarabanda* and the *chacona* in the seventeenth century; a little later came the *bolero*, the *cachuca*, the *canario*, the *cucaracha*, the *cumbé*, the *dingo*, the *fandango*, the *guaracha*, the *guineo*, the *jaleo*, the *jopeo*, the *mandingoy*, the *tirana*, the *zarambeque*, the *zerengue*, the *zorongo*, among many others. These dances interpreted by eighteenth-century Gypsies are of very diverse origins: Andalusia, the Canaries, Africa and the Americas. The *guineo* and the *mandingoy* clearly display their African

Parish festival, Valencia
1862

origins, as does the *cumbé*, whose refrain evokes
Angola; the *guaracha* is Cuban and the *bolero* has two
distinct identities: the version that appeared in Cadiz in
the eighteenth century has a very Iberian form and a three-part rhythm,
while the version that surged through Europe the following century is dis-
tinctly Cuban.

What became of all these musical styles? The most ancient of them
were preserved in the bosom of Gitano families, where they underwent
some very strange transformations, as we shall see. The others all died
out, with the exception of the *fandango*, and the *bolero* which, as already
noted, was soon to re-emerge in another form.

Instruments

Quite apart from the theatre, where actors in Gypsy costume performed so-called 'Gypsy' music and dance, we also know a great deal about the participation of real Gypsies in public and private festivities. The essential element of the performance was always the dance, with musical accompaniment usually limited to percussion: a fairly large, slender tambourine (known as a *pandero* or *pandereta*) made of wooden hoops fitted with small metallic jingles (*sonajas*) and sometimes covered with skin on one or both sides. This basic instrument was sometimes supplemented by a guitar and, more frequently, castanets or perhaps strings of tiny bells around the dancers' ankles. Gitano women usually danced in groups of eight, and always outnumbered male dancers.

The really remarkable thing about these performances – whether real ones on the streets during festivals, or imitations on theatre stages – is that, despite official prohibitions, their popularity continued to grow even as anti-Gypsy prejudice and persecution intensified. This situation may appear paradoxical, but it provides an excellent illustration of the ever-ambiguous attitudes of sedentary populations towards the Gypsy people, a mixture of fear and envy, hatred and fascination.

Spain and the Gypsies: a policy of forced settlement

G ypsies began to make their way into Spain from 1425, via the Pyrenees. To begin with, they travelled in small groups of some thirty to a hundred individuals, under the direction of leaders calling themselves 'counts' or 'dukes' in order to impress the local authorities. They claimed to have been driven out of their own country, Little Egypt – a region of Messenia in the south-eastern Peloponnese – by Turkish invaders, and to have been ordered by the Pope to complete seven years of pilgrimage. With this double status as refugees expelled for their faith, and as Christian pilgrims, they were generally well received, and monarchs granted them letters of protection. In May 1425, for example, King Alphonsus V of Aragon intervened on behalf of Count Thomas of Little Egypt, en route to Santiago de Compostela, from whom the inhabitants of the city of Alagon had stolen two magnificent hounds. In 1462, two counts of Little Egypt were accorded a princely welcome by Constable Miguel Lucas de Iranzo, who invited them to dine at his table and provided accommodation for the rest of their troupe – some one hundred persons – in his palace at Jaén, in Andalusia, for a fortnight. Some years later, in 1470, the same constable received a count and a duke of Little Egypt at his Andujar residence, in the same manner.

From 1480, more troupes of Gypsies arrived in Spain. The men leading them no longer called themselves counts or dukes, but 'knights' or 'captains'. Nor did they mention Little Egypt, saying only that they came from Greece. The memory of this division of Gypsies into two groups was to survive in Spain at least until the early seventeenth century: in 1618 a scholar, Salazar of Mendoza, informs us that the 'Greeks' are blacksmiths while the 'Egyptians' are more closely associated with horse-dealing, the women distinguished from their 'Greek' counterparts

Safe-conduct granted by Ferdinand the Catholic to Philip, Count of Little Egypt, at Seville, March 1491

by characteristic costume including a multi-coloured blanket pinned at the shoulder and a great round headdress.

The intolerance of the Catholic monarchs* and their successors

With the instatement of the Catholic monarchs, intolerance reared its head in Spain, a country where three religions – Christian, Jewish and Muslim – had until then co-existed. The Inquisition, set up in 1478, was to harry converted Jews (known as *Conversos* or *Marranos*) before turning its attentions to the *Morisques* or Moors (former Muslims forcibly converted to Christianity) and Protestants. 1492, the year of the reconquest of Grenada* and the discovery of the New World, was also the year the Jews were expelled. Then, in 1499, three years prior to the forced conversion of the Muslims, Ferdinand V and Isabella I, joint monarchs of Aragon and Castile, signed Spain's first anti-Gypsy law. This opens with the gracious salutation,

> To you, the Egyptians, who wander our Kingdoms and Domains with your women, your children and your families, Salutation and Grace!

It ends, by contrast, on a less amiable note: the Gypsies were given a sixty-day period in which to settle down and take up a trade or hire themselves out as servants. Those who refused the proposal were given a further sixty days in which to quit the country permanently, on pain of one hundred lashes and condemnation to perpetual exile. In case of recidivism, they were to have their ears slit (the contemporary equivalent of 'having a record'), be incarcerated in chains for a period of sixty days, then re-expelled. Finally, if they persisted in disobeying, they were to become the slaves for life of whoever captured them.

This appalling text (adapted by the poet Felix Grande and interpreted by the Gitano singer Juan Peña 'El Lebrijano' in a celebrated 1979 recording under the title of *Persecution*) appears to have had little impact at the time. Forty years on, in 1539, after many complaints from the States General* (*las Cortes**) of Castile, Charles I* decided to issue a new law. This time, Gypsies were given a three-month deadline in which to choose between settlement and exile: once it had elapsed, any male aged between twenty and fifty caught travelling in a group of three or more was to be sent to the galleys* for six years.

There is evidence that these later measures were indeed enforced since, six years later, when mutiny broke out on a galley ship, there were

Warrant for the arrest of a Gypsy woman, Maria Rodriguez, issued by the Toledo Inquisition, dated 20 July 1631

thirty Gypsies aboard, three of them nearing the end of their sentences. Nonetheless the Gypsies must have succeeded in adapting to these curious interdictions on travelling in groups as, in 1560, Philip II in his turn signed another law, this one specifying that all men of the Gypsy community caught on the roads were to be sent to the galleys even if travelling in a group of less than three at the time of their arrest. This time round, the women were not forgotten: those wearing their traditional costume were to be whipped and banished for life.

'There is no such thing as a gypsy'

The laws of Castile, aimed at the immediate settlement of the Gypsy population, were somewhat original in comparison to those of the rest of Europe and indeed the remainder of Spain, which, deeming nomads to be undesirables, contented themselves with their regular expulsion. This difference of treatment was to have considerable repercussions later on, as we shall see, since the Gitanos were to experience mass settlement over the course of the eighteenth century, in stark contrast to the situation of Gypsies elsewhere in Europe.

The Spaniards hesitated somewhat before arriving at their particular 'solution', however. If settlement remained the official policy, there were still a fair number of proponents of expulsion pure and simple, and these expressed themselves loudest in the States General. In fact every party sought the most efficient method of ridding the country of a group whose mobility disturbed the more sedentary populations. It did not seem wise to send Gypsies over a border that they would simply re-cross when their new hosts' intolerance levels rose in their turn. Moreover, Spanish policy towards the Gypsy minority was based on a peculiar concept which can be summed up as 'There is no such thing as a Gypsy'.

This idea was based on the writings of some sixteenth century scholars, such as Albert Krantz and Sebastian Münster, who claimed that Gypsies were perfectly willing to accept into their troupes individuals from the countries they passed through. Spurred by mistrust and hatred, the scholars had concluded that the Gypsies were not an ethnically distinct people, but a ragbag of vagabonds fearing neither God nor man, the 'dregs of the nations' as one of them put it.

The Spanish were eager to develop this hypothesis, particularly following the expulsion of the Moors during the seventeenth century. Some went so far as to claim that Gypsies dyed their skin each month with the

juice of certain plants, in order to appear foreign, and that they had made
up a bogus language, a sort of incomprehensible argot, towards the same
end. We shall look into how subsequent Spanish law was built around
such thinking, and how the denial of Gypsy ethnicity led the Spanish into
relentless suppression of every manifestation of distinctiveness, such as
language, costume, lifestyle and traditional trades.

Recipes for extermination

However the Gypsy minority was defined, be it as an ethnic minority of
foreign origin or as a subculture consisting of local drop-outs, the primary
objective was their elimination or, as official texts sometimes phrased it,
to *exterminate* them. As we have seen, deportation was not always considered to be the most efficacious way of achieving this, and many
Spaniards felt that the ideal approach would be to have this odd section of
the population disappear into the masses of ordinary citizenry. The first
step, obviously, was to prevent Gypsies from breeding, and in 1594 two
deputies to the States General of Castile came up with a rather original
approach to this subject. According to them, all that was needed was to
make the men live in a province very far from the one where women
would be obliged to reside, and of course to prohibit both from travelling.
Speaking their own language and wearing distinctive clothing were also
to be forbidden. In this way, they would have no option but to marry the
good peasants of their respective regions, and the problem would very
quickly be solved.

The Assembly was divided on this proposal. A majority leaned
towards expulsion, arguing that the supposedly very large numbers of
'false Gypsies' would doubtless prefer to renounce their way of life rather
than be run out of their own country, and that the numbers actually
expelled would therefore be negligible. Others, by contrast, felt that
deportation was ineffectual against a nomadic people and that it would be
better to send every one of them to the galleys. This latter solution was in
fact largely implemented, with mass arrests of Gypsies decreed throughout the course of the seventeenth century whenever the Navy required
new hands on the oars.

In 1610, when the general expulsion of the Moors had begun, the
Duke of Lerme and the Council of State considered applying the same
method to the Gypsies, but preferred first to complete the expulsion of
the former Muslims, whose conversion was felt to be superficial. The

Gypsy project was eventually abandoned, despite numerous and violent protests.

The solution ultimately adopted by the government was the dispersal of Gypsies among cities of a thousand or more inhabitants, where they were to be kept under close scrutiny, with any manifestation of distinctive characteristics expressly prohibited. This project, adopted by the States General that same year, 1610, was to inspire all subsequent law. Its basic premise was the argument that the Gypsies are not a *nation*, or, to put it another way, do not comprise a separate ethnic group.

The law of Philip IV, 1633

Despite numerous petitions in favour of expulsion (all driven by implacable racial hatred and signed by scholars such as Salazar de Mendoza, university professors such as Sancho de Moncada, and court judges such as Juan de Quiñones) or arguing that the mere fact of being a Gypsy was a crime that ought to rate the galleys, the law signed by Philip IV in 1633 held true to the 1610 States General proposal and declared outright:

> Those who call themselves Gypsies are not so by origin or nature, but solely because they have adopted this way of life, with measurable harmful effects and absence of profit for the State.

In consequence, Gypsies were banned from speaking a language or wearing costume different from those of other Spaniards. Horse-dealing and trading at fairs – their principal means of livelihood – were also forbidden them. The first article of this law very clearly reveals its ultimate goal: to submerge a conspicuous minority within the broad masses, thus obliterating it. To this end, Gypsies were ordered to quit areas where they lived together, in order to be dispersed into the population at large. They were forbidden to associate, whether publicly or in secret. They were kept under strict surveillance, with particular attention devoted to ensuring that they did not meet or marry among themselves; their religious practices were also closely monitored.

Article 2 applied itself to expunging the very name and memory of the cursed race (or subculture, depending on the point of view). Gypsy or not, no one was to have the right to utter this name, henceforward regarded as a grave insult and thus subject to heavy sanctions. All Gypsy entertainments, whether authentic or theatrical imitations, were prohibited:

> Be it in the form of dances or any other occasion, no action or representa-
> tion will be tolerated; the costume and the name of the Gypsies are to be
> forbidden.

Article 3 outlined the extremely severe sanctions to be applied to Gypsies
daring to leave their places of residence: once again, the penalty was to be
slavery for life. Gypsies caught in possession of weapons were to be sentenced to eight years in the galleys.

Gypsy hunting and ecclesiastical immunity

The adopted policy of assimilation of the Gypsy people was to be gradually perfected right up to the mid-eighteenth century. In parallel with it,
police measures aimed at any Gypsies still wandering the countryside
were reinforced. Within a short period armed militias specialising in this
hunting down of humans were formed. In many regions, particularly La
Mancha and Estremadura, bounty-hunters levied small troupes of armed
cavalry to scour the countryside for Gypsies and deliver up to justice any
they came across – dead or alive. They hoped to win honours in recognition of their actions, but above all they did it for the substantial benefits
to be gained through confiscating Gypsy goods as well as extorting fines
from local judicial administrators, whom they declared guilty of negli-
gence or complicity. *Santa Hermandad* ('The Holy Brotherhood'), the
armed league created in 1476 by the Catholic Monarchs, operated along
the same lines, so effectively indeed that numerous conflicts arose
between these para-militias and the ordinary forces of the law on the one
hand, and Church jurisdiction on the other. In 1738, for example, an
*alcalde** of Zalamea – a city whose resistance to abuses of power had
already been made famous in plays by Lope de Vega and Calderón –
confronted *Hermandad* archers in defence of Gypsies living in the
municipality.

The question of ecclesiastical jurisdiction was to be a bone of con-
tention for over a century. From 1643 Pedro de Villalobos, Dean of the
Faculty of Law at the University of Salamanca, orchestrated a campaign
aimed at demonstrating that the right to sanctuary, under which anyone
pursued by the secular authorities could take refuge in churches, monas-
teries and convents, should not apply to Gypsies.

In 1700 the issue was revived with a trial calling so-called 'cold
immunity' (*iglesias frías**) into question. Once an alleged offender had
been removed by secular law enforcement agents from a church or other

Privileges of the Santa Hermandad, issued in 1721

venue under ecclesiastical jurisdiction and tried, he had to be returned to the place from which he had been arrested. If the authorities failed to do this, the individual could continue to appeal to the Church if rearrested or implicated in new offences. The Council* of Castile declared itself scandalised by such practices and formulated various proposals for submission to the Vatican with a view to their eradication.

In 1721 a commission was specially created by Philip IV to determine whether ecclesiastical immunity applied to Gypsies, and the question was definitively resolved in 1748 following an accord with the Holy See authorising the transfer of Gypsies claiming sanctuary in churches to chapels within the grounds of enclosed penal colonies. This measure, which stripped Gypsies of their last protection, was to facilitate the general internment carried out the following year.

The laws of forced assimilation, 1695, 1717, 1745 and 1746

Settlement in closely supervised places of residence was seen as a first step towards the elimination of the Gypsies through assimilation. Numerous laws were passed to supplement the measures of the 1633 Pragmatic*. The first of these, signed by Charles II in 1695, aimed to remedy the failures of all earlier legislation. Its key measures were as follows:

Article 1: All Gypsies were required to register with the authorities of their place of residence within thirty days, declaring their name, age, marital status, profession, names and ages of children (if any), as well as weapons, horses, mules and other animals in their possession.

Article 2: Those who failed to register, or who failed to make a complete declaration, were liable to six years in the galleys.

Article 3: Following a period of a further thirty days, all Gypsies must be gone from the country, under pain of eight years in the galleys for men and two hundred lashes for women. Only Gypsies domiciled within communities of 200 or more inhabitants, under conditions enumerated in the following articles, would be tolerated.

Article 4: The sole occupation authorised for Gypsies was the cultivation of the soil. All infractions were punishable by eight years in the galleys.

Article 5: It was forbidden for Gypsies to possess or make use of horses. Only donkeys and mules essential for field labour would be tolerated.

Article 6: It was forbidden to possess firearms on pain of 200 lashes and eight years in the galleys.

Article 10: The buying, selling and trading of animals of all kinds was forbidden, on pain of six years in the galleys.

Article 11: Gypsies might not live together in the same quarter, nor wear costume distinct from that of other inhabitants, nor speak their own language, on pain of six years in the galleys for men, 100 lashes and deportation for women.

Article 12: Gypsies might leave their place of residence only to go to work in the fields. They might not travel to another locality without written authorisation.

Article 13: The galley penalties mentioned in the preceding articles applied to male Gypsies aged between seventeen and sixty years. Boys between fourteen and seventeen were to be sent to forced labour, while women were to be punished by whipping and banishment.

Article 14: Any Gypsy, settled or not, who travelled with two or more companions and possessed a weapon would be condemned to death, even if not caught in the act.

The 1717 law is merely an amended version of the above. From now on, any Gypsy found in possession of a firearm, whatever the circumstances, was to be subject to the death penalty. Article 4, stipulating agriculture as the sole occupation authorised to Gypsies, was revised to specify blacksmithing as particularly prohibited to them. Finally, its principal novelty lies in its designating forty-one cities as the sole authorised places of residence for Gypsies.

PRAGMATICA:
QVE SV MAGESTAD MANDA
publicar, dando la forma en que deven vivir
los Gitanos que se hallaren en estos Reynos,
con expresion de las penas en que
incurren contraviniendo
à ella.

Año   1695.

CON LICENCIA.

En Madrid : Por Julian de Paredes,
Impressor de Libros, en la Plaçuela
del Angel.

The Pragmatic of Charles II,
12 June 1695

The law of October 1745 is exclusively concerned with Gypsies who desert their places of residence. Those who failed to return within a fortnight were declared to be bandits and could be shot on sight with no further legal process required.

As for the law of 1746, this adds a further thirty-four cities to the 1717 list, and specifies that Gypsies are to be distributed at a ratio of one family per hundred inhabitants. The authorities were to ensure that there was no more than one Gypsy family in any given street or quarter, and were charged with supervising these families' lifestyle and activities, taking particular care to keep them separated from each other.

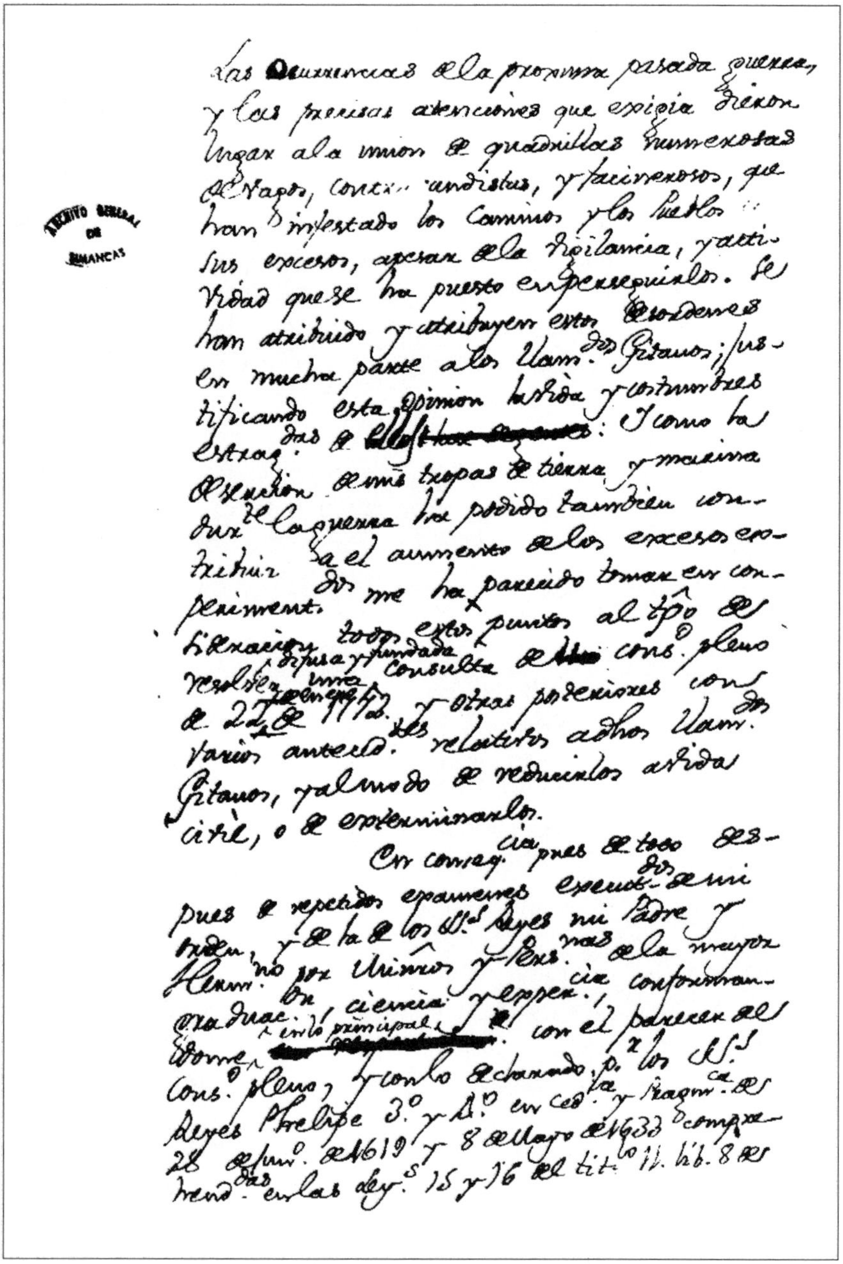

ARCHIVO GENERAL DE SIMANCAS

Las ocurrencias de la proxima pasada guerra,
y las precisas atenciones que exigia dieron
lugar a la union de quadrillas numerosas
de vagos, contrabandistas, y facinerosos, que
han infestado los Caminos y los Pueblos
sus excesos, apesar de la vigilancia, y acti-
vidad que se ha puesto en perseguirlos. Se
han atribuido y atribuyen estos desordenes
en mucha parte a los llamados Gitanos; jus-
tificando esta opinion la vida y costumbres
estragadas de [illegible]: Y como la
ocupacion de mis tropas de tierra y marina
durante la guerra ha podido tambien con-
tribuir a el aumento de los excesos ex-
perimentados me ha parecido tomar en con-
sideracion todos estos puntos al tiempo de
resolver una consulta del cons.o pleno
de 22 de [illegible] 1772 y otras posteriores con
varios antecedentes relativos a dichos llamados
Gitanos, y al modo de reducirlos a vida
civil, o de exterminarlos.
En consequencia pues de todo despues de repetidos examenes executados de mi
orden, y de la de los Reyes mi Padre y
Hermano por Ministros y Personas de la mayor
graduacion, ciencia y experiencia, conformandome
[illegible] con el parecer del
Consejo pleno, y con lo declarado por los Reyes
Phelipe 3.o y 4.o en ced.a y pragm.ca de
28 de Junio de 1619 y 8 de Mayo de 1633 compre-
hendidas en las leyes 15 y 16 del tit.o 11 lib. 8 de

Manuscript of the Pragmatic of 19 September 1783

The general internment of 1749

Once these measures concerning the dispersal and settlement of Gypsies in a limited number of closely supervised localities (seventy-five in all) had been implemented, and the right to sanctuary abolished, after negotiations with Rome in 1748, the scene was set for radical action. Many must have felt that the process of total elimination through assimilation was taking far too long to produce appreciable results, and that the time had come to employ more effective methods.

As a result, the Bishop of Oviedo, Governor of the Council, who had been developing a programme for the mass arrest of Gypsies in Spain since 1747, was able to put his plan into action. King Ferdinand VI hesitated at first, but eventually agreed to it. As yet unresolved was the question of what was to become of the Gypsies once they had been arrested. The Bishop put forward two proposals: the first was their general expulsion with the execution of the recalcitrant; the second, general incarceration, with all prisoners put to forced labour. This latter proposal was eventually adopted. Able-bodied men between fifteen and fifty were sent to forced labour in the arsenals*, while boys aged twelve to fifteen were pressed into the Navy.

Another problem was the need for secrecy, not to mention the logistics of implementing mass arrests at the same hour of the same night throughout the whole of Spain. In fact the whole process had to be repeated for Gypsies who were not domiciled in official places of residence.

These measures drew a storm of protest as soon as they were implemented. There were complaints from the Gypsies themselves, as yet unaware that theirs was a collective life sentence, demanding to know why they had been arrested when living peacefully in their own homes. Local authorities in the Gypsy municipalities also objected, since, despite the laws, many Gypsies occupied key positions in local businesses or crafts, and many communities suddenly found themselves without a blacksmith to repair agricultural tools, a miller to crush the oil from the olive harvest, or even a baker. The most sustained protests came from the directors of the arsenals, utterly swamped by the arrival of thousands of convicts who had to be chained up at night in decommissioned ships or crammed into warehouses where they risked suffocation through overcrowding. What is more, no one knew exactly what to do with the prisoners since, despite being seriously weakened by the conditions of their detention, they were meant to replace existing labourers carrying out harbour construction and maintenance – transporting extremely heavy stones while up to their waists in mud and water and encumbered by enormous leg chains.

Officials in charge of these establishments feared epidemics and mutiny. In fact mortality was high, but escape bids were rare and quickly brought in hand. Nonetheless the king eventually realised that an injustice had been perpetrated and ordered the release of all Gypsies deemed to be honest: their original places of residence were to reclaim them by honouring their requests for certificates of good conduct. Yet, according to a report issued by La Carraca Arsenal on 29 December 1749, less than half the internees benefited from this concession. In fact the intendant of Cartagena claimed shortly afterwards that those released were not necessarily the best, but simply the poorest, since municipal authorities were none too anxious to return the substantial assets confiscated from the well-to-do at the time of their arrest. Some of these unhappy victims were to rot in prison for up to sixteen years. In effect, the order for the Gypsies' general release, given by Charles III in 1763, was to be greatly delayed by the two Council Prosecutors, Campomanes and Sierra Cienfuegos, who, instead of designating places of residence for liberated internees as requested, became embroiled in endless arguments.

A dark age of enlightenment

The great debate raging around the Gypsies in the second half of this so-called 'enlightened' century is of little credit to the illustrious men involved, admirers of the French Encyclopaedists, such as the Count of Campomanes, Prosecutor of the Council of Castile, and the Count of Aranda, a personal friend of d'Alembert and Voltaire and President of the same Council. The former proposed the incarceration of all able-bodied settled Gypsies in penal colonies, which he euphemistically dubbed 'closed residences'; all others were simply to be deported to America. The Count of Aranda championed deportation for unmarried Gypsies.

He stipulated that boys should be sent to the islands and girls to the mainland, thus reviving the method of extermination proposed by the States General in 1594. As for married couples of childbearing age, Aranda argued simply that there should not be more than one such couple per locality; anyone straying over a quarter of a league (less than two kilometres) from their domicile would be condemned to the gallows, whilst children would be separated from their parents at weaning, or when they began to talk. Charles III, whom posterity was to take as the very model of an enlightened sovereign, went further still: he wanted Gypsy children to be removed from their parents at birth, and opposed their being sent to school, particularly in the case of girls, since he felt that mixing with boys (there were very few girls' schools at the time) would only encourage their natural licentiousness.

The law of 1783

This debate eventually led to the passing of the last of the Spanish Gypsy laws. Signed in 1783 by Charles III, it was drawn up by Campomanes in collaboration with a far less prominent Councillor, Pedro Valiente. The deportation and 'closed residences' dear to the former were finally dropped and the amendments concerning children, proposed by Aranda and indeed the king himself, were modified and limited to the families of persistent offenders. In fact the principal novelty of this law was that it granted Gypsies equal rights with other citizens, in particular with regard to work and residence. Article 1 reiterates the principle of the 1663 law: *'Those who call themselves Gypsies are not so by origin or nature,'* but adds an important proviso: *'and they do not spring from corrupt stock.'* In other words, there was to be no more talk of an infamous or cursed race – but by the same token any manifestation of distinctiveness, be it language, costume or lifestyle, was to be severely penalised.

Article 3 states that the word *Gypsy* and its substitute *New Castilian** have become very grave insults, the use of which will henceforward be proscribed. Article 5 allows ex-Gypsies (now unnameable) access to all trades and guilds, on condition, obviously, that they renounce all distinguishing characteristics. By contrast the recalcitrant who continue to comport themselves as Gypsies are to be branded with red-hot irons, and, in case of recidivism, condemned to death.

Despite its limitations, the law of 1783 did effectively confer some freedoms on the Gypsies, now permitted to exercise the occupation of their choice and reside wherever they liked. Indeed, considerable movement took place over the following years, and shortly after the death of Charles III, in 1788, more or less as the French Revolution was getting under way, the first families of Gypsy horse-dealers from Barcelona and thereabouts began to cross the frontier and establish themselves in Southern France.

CHAPTER THREE

Gypsy-Andalusians: the 'flamenco families'

The last chapter outlined the official situation of the Gypsies in Spain from their arrival in the fifteenth century to the passing of the law of 1783, a period marked by a long series of assimilative measures. What these laws do not tell us is that some Gypsy families were to settle spontaneously in certain towns and villages – especially in Andalusia – outside the implacable surveillance of the officially approved residences. Sometimes this was by their own initiative, before draconian laws

Gypsy women of Triana, a suburb of Seville

regulating settlement came into operation, sometimes because they enjoyed particular privileges there.

The Moorish heritage

Historians have frequently confused the Moors (Spanish Muslims subjected to forcible conversion from 1502) and the Gypsies. Many nineteenth and early twentieth century authors asserted that the Gypsies were descended from Arabs. More recently a hypothesis emerged which claimed that the Moors disguised themselves *en masse* as Gypsies to evade the general expulsion of the early seventeenth century. This hypothesis quickly gained widespread acceptance and has been used by other authors towards unabashedly racist ends, the aim being to demonstrate definitively that the families of Lower Andalusia, among whom the flamenco phenomenon came into being in the early nineteenth century, were not Gypsy.

This hypothesis rests on rather slender evidence, namely two Inquisition trials and a certain similarity between the characteristic trades exercised by the two communities which, as we shall see, lends itself to a simpler explanation. The first of these trials, before the Inquisition of Grenada in 1577, was of Fernando López, a Moor, arrested because he was taken for a Gypsy. His disguise seems most unlikely to have been in order to avoid deportation (since this project wasn't even on the cards until 1582, and was only implemented between 1609 and 1615); in fact López was en route to North Africa at the time of his arrest. The second trial, conducted before the Inquisition of Valencia in 1590, is even less conclusive, since it concerns one Pedro Orejón who 'became Gypsy' for the love of a beautiful Gypsy girl. There are many such cases of conversion for love, in which neither the fact of being Moorish nor the threat of expulsion are of relevance.

The similarity of occupations can be logically explained by the fact that many Gypsies took advantage of the expulsions to fill the resulting gaps. The Gypsies were also to be subject to general expulsion once the Moorish project had been concluded, but this plan was eventually dropped. In 1763 Campomanes furnishes us with an *a posteriori* explanation for this decision:

> Expelling citizens from the Country was not good policy, since when the Moors were driven out in 1613, in considerable numbers, they left behind them deserted houses and fields, and abandoned trades.

The Council Prosecutor adds that there was more to be gained by encouraging Gypsies to replace the deportees, and that besides some did so spontaneously, with no particular incentive other than the wish to avoid mounting persecution and achieve a degree of security.

This is the explanation for the fact that many Gypsy families, particularly in Andalusia, exercise trades and crafts generally scorned by *Old Christians* (people of Spanish stock) and practised by the Moors up to the seventeenth century. These include not only blacksmithing and horse-dealing – which are in any case traditional Gypsy trades – but also masonry, shoemaking, rope- and mat-weaving, baking and butchery, among others.

The first settled families

This quiet integration of Gypsy families was in fact already going on well before the departure of the Moors. In 1573, many expelled Gypsy families requested readmission to the Navarra villages of Falces and Larraga. Thanks to the service records of some of their members, who had fought with valour under the command of Don Juan of Austria during the Moorish revolt (1569-1570), they were readmitted, despite opposition from residents. All the same, they were required to abandon their language and costume, and to avoid the company of other Gypsies.

It was in 1576, only a very few years later, that the Cortés and Medrano families settled in Antequera, Andalusia. Some twenty years later, as it became more and more difficult for Gypsies to travel the roads of Spain, they applied through the intermediary of the local authorities for a royal pass authorising them to travel freely in pursuit of their trades. Nine witnesses, including two priests, four municipal councillors and a lawyer, testified on their behalf, and this is how we now know that these families were good Christians, dressed like everybody else, owned property in the town and sent their children to school. They were, in fact, indistinguishable from other inhabitants: they were socially integrated, they cultivated their lands, and paid their taxes. Moreover they too had service records, as they helped to defend the cities of Cadiz and Gibraltar when these were under English and Dutch attack, and had also supplied grain to the Army, the border defence forces and the Fleet.

'Old Castilian' certificates

There are a fair number of similar cases, where Gypsy families obtained royal Privileges* in the form of certification officially granting them *Old Castilian* status and exempting them from current anti-Gypsy legislation. One of the most interesting is that of the Bustamante, Rocamora, Montoya and Flores families, who procured a royal warrant at Valladolid (then the Court Residence) in 1602, a second letter in 1620, and a further royal warrant in 1623. The records tell us that they or their near relatives – fathers, brothers, brothers-in-law and nephews – had served with the army in Flanders for a total of twenty-four years, and that many had given their lives for Spain. Consequently the king granted them the right to choose their place of domicile and to trade at fairs and markets despite existing anti-Gypsy law, from which they were exempted.

Recent research, such as that carried out in Andalusia by Manuel Martinez, confirms that the number of Gypsies involved in the war with Flanders was 'much higher than estimated heretofore'. Martinez cites the case histories of many Andalusian Gypsies who were Flanders veterans, among them Sebastián de Maldonado and Sebastián de Soto. In 1639 each of these men offered to recruit, in Seville and elsewhere in Andalusia, a company of 200 men of their own community (*nación*), with whom they would return to the battlefields. It should be noted that the families of these Gypsy soldiers customarily followed the army and that mixed marriages probably took place during their long stays in Flanders; some claim that this could account for the significant numbers of blond, blue-eyed Andalusian Gypsies. Be that as it may, the return of the Flanders veterans between the Treaty of the Pyrenees (1659) and the Treaty of Utrecht (1713) coincided with a spectacular upsurge in the persecution of Gypsies and it is reasonable to suppose that those with service records would have used them to protect themselves, preferring to pass as Flemish (*Flamencos*) than as Gypsies. Moreover, when we trace the histories of the families most closely involved in the Flanders war, we note that they are intermarried with most of the flamenco families. Indeed, some of the most reknowned flamenco families – the Flores, Montoyas and Sotos – have been demonstrated to descend directly from Flanders veterans, and new discoveries will undoubtedly add further names to this list.

Changes in a privileged situation

Even for the privileged, things have a tendency to go awry. A Gypsy woman named María de Montoya, who had obtained a letter from the Council in 1677 authorising her to reside in a number of towns and villages, ran into difficulties three years later with *Santa Hermandad** archers, as well as with the authorities in her place of domicile. When she applied for a fresh copy in 1692 to replace the now badly worn original, the Council refused, on the grounds that she was simply using the document as a permit for vagabondage. Similarly, in the early eighteenth century the González family, domiciled at Brihuega and subsequently at Valdepeñas, were to suffer persecution, despite holding numerous letters from the Council requesting that they be treated as *Old Castilians*.

Saved by their music

In certain cities increasingly restrictive anti-Gypsy laws posed problems for the authorities. This was the case in 1698 in Seville, where Gypsies played the tambourine and fife free of charge for companies of the militia. The grateful town wished to spare them from persecution, especially as they were also blacksmiths: the new law, passed three years earlier, barred them from all but agricultural labour. The Council granted the Seville municipal authorities' request by permitting them to make an exception for these Gypsy musicians.

Official recognition of the Gypsies' contribution to society

After 1717 things became even more complicated, as Gypsies no longer had the right to reside outside those cities expressly designated by law. For a time, families who had become well integrated thanks to their professions, continued to lead a trouble-free existence since the local authorities were not always fully aware of legislative developments in the capital. Yet the Council was implacable: the 1717 law was reiterated in 1726, 1731, 1738 and 1740. In 1746, as explained earlier, the number of approved residences was raised from forty-one to seventy-five, and the authorities in those towns which were not on the list started to become uneasy. At Jerez the *corregidor** and Municipal Council jointly intervened on behalf of a number of families by the name of Monje (one of whose descendants, living at San Fernando near Cadiz, was to become famous in our own times as *Camarón*). Their statement attested that the Monjes had been living in Jerez for many generations, that they were employed in agriculture and at blacksmithing (which was illegal, but the authors appeared to be unaware of this), and that they were very useful to the farmers' guild. In consequence, they desired that the Monjes remain in Jerez and not be subjected to the new law (on the understanding that they would not wear the costume of the Gypsies, speak their language, or mix with them). Similarly, the *corregidor* of Motril intervened on behalf of the Cortés, de Arroyo, de Cárcamo, de Carmona, Belmúdez and Torcu-ato families, as these were employed in local sugar refineries, then at the height of operations.

At Vélez-Malaga, the *corregidor* interceded in favour of sixteen Gypsy families who had been living in the town for several generations and whose work as blacksmiths and sheep-shearers – both expressly forbidden occupations – was deemed highly useful to the community. His statement included a plea for recognition of the fact that they had obtained authorisation to reside in the town, and that obliging them to leave their work and move elsewhere would threaten their very survival. Having studied the various cases put before them, the Council granted the *corregidors* permission to keep their Gypsies, provided that they behaved, in every particular, like any other citizens. Having made this decision, the Council planned to extend this type of exemption to all localities requesting it, on condition that the Gypsies concerned, recognised as fulfilling a role of public usefulness, had resided in their locality for a minimum of ten years. As for Gypsies in possession of papers authorising them to be classified as *Old Castilians*, many of which had been confiscated during enforced relocation, the Council decided to return these to their owners, provided they too fulfilled the same conditions. The aim was to avoid the pointless overcrowding of the approved residences with families whose presence was considered beneficial elsewhere.

All this time preparations were under way for the great round-up of 1749. Initially, no one was to be spared, though, as we have seen, some privileged individuals and their families were 'reclaimed' by their places of residence a few months later. Until 1783 most Spanish Gypsies were kept under close surveillance, but we may assume that some well-integrated families, recognised as useful in their Andalusian villages, were less dramatically affected than the rest of the community.

After 1783

The tumult continued throughout Spain for a good five years after the passing of Charles III's law in 1783. Many *corregidors*, accustomed to thinking of Gypsies as outlaws, or indeed as simple gallows fodder, were unwilling to see them regaining even a degree of liberty. In practice the Pragmatic was almost always interpreted negatively, and arrests actually increased. In 1785 an *alcalde* went so far as to write to the Count of Floridablanca, Minister of State and Counsellor to Charles III, to propose the systematic arrest of all transient strangers for an identity-check, and requiring all Gypsies wishing to travel outside their place of residence to carry a special pass. Restrictive clauses reminiscent of these even reappeared in the regulations of the *Guardia Civil*, drawn up in 1943 under the Franco regime:

Article 4: The Gypsies are to be kept under scrupulous surveillance, the documents in their possession examined with the greatest of attention, their clothing closely observed, their way of life monitored, and all other measures taken which will make it possible to form a clear picture of their activities as well as the motive and destination of their travels.

Article 5: Given that individuals in this category are generally of no fixed abode and are continually on the move from place to place to avoid recognition, it is advisable to gather all relevant information about them in order to prevent their stealing horses or goods of any other type.

At the same time it should be noted that not all reports submitted to the Council and the king after the passing of the 1783 Pragmatic were negative. Some courts reported that offences committed by Gypsies over the previous ten years were generally of a petty nature, primarily the theft of foodstuffs, a fact which would seem to indicate that the perpetrators stole from necessity. Magistrates also remarked on the tendency to systematically attribute to the Gypsies all thefts committed in an area, and the fact that many *Payos* (non-Gypsies) took advantage of this situation to hide their own misdeeds.

The censuses of 1784 and 1785

The legislation drafted by Campomanes and Valiente in 1771 called for a

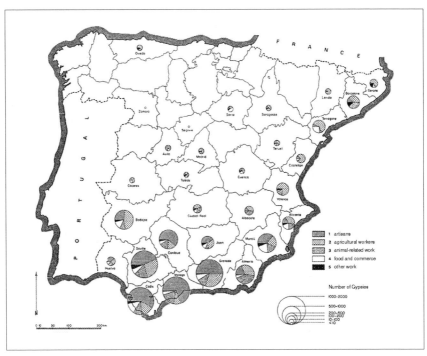

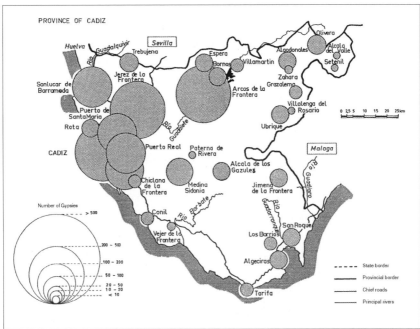

Maps of Spain and of the province of Cadiz showing geographical distribution of the Gypsy population

PLAN GENERAL

en que con difinicion de Partidos y Provincias se manifiesta el numero de personas conocidas con el nombre de Gitanos que se hallan establecidas en los Reynos de la Corona de Castilla, con expresion de los avecindados antes de la R.l Pragmática de 19. de Septiembre de 1783: de los que lo han executado despues; y de los contraventores castigados y presos segun resulta de las listas remitidas por los Corregidores y Alcaldes mayores à consecuencia de lo mandado por S. M. en R.l Orn de 20. de Diz.e de 1784 que se les comunicó en 28 del mismo

PROVINCIAS	PARTIDOS	Gitanos avecindados antes de la Pragmática				Gitanos avecindados despues de la Pragmática				Contraventores		Total de personas por lo correspondiente à cada Partido	Total de personas por lo correspondiente à cada Provincia
		Varones de mas de 17 años	Hembras de mas de 17 años	Varones de menos de 17 años	Hembras de menos de 17 años	Varones de mas de 17 años	Hembras de mas de 17 años	Varones de menos de 17 años	Hembras de menos de 17 años	Castigados	Presos y perdidos las causas		
Avila	Avila	3	7	7	3							20	20
Cordova	Cordova	10	16	11	12	2	1				1	53	474
	Lucena	107	121	56	88	4	5	4	2		1	418	
Cuenca	Cuenca	8	10	4	5	6	8	2	1		3	40	123
	Requena					11	13	4	6			33	
	San Clemente	5	3	5		11	13	4				33	
Estremadura	Alcantara	10	16	12	7	1	1					52	631
	Almendralejo	4	3	1	2							11	
	Caceres	1		1	1				1			4	
	Badajoz	58	46	18	25	10	7	7	6			177	
	Hornachos	3	3			3	1					6	
	Llerena	40	55	25	30	3	3	3	2		3	172	
	Merida	33	29	27	26	1	1	1				120	
	Segura de Leon	2		1								3	
	Trujillo					1	1					2	
	Villanueva de la Serena	1		2	11	4		5				32	
	Xerez de los Cavalleros	13	7	6	6							32	
Granada	Adra	16	14	14	14	7	8	6	5			86	2032
	Alhama	15	17	11								52	
	Almeria	46	70	36	20	12	10	2				186	
	Almuñecar	24	24	16	12	2	4	1	2			86	
	Baza	127	105	77	83	32	23	31	24	1	3	512	
	Egüena	5	2	2								11	
	Guadix	182	153	114	23	10	7	10	2		11	580	
	Loxa	32	35	25	21	12	13	21	2		1	174	
	Vega de Malaga	16	20	12	15	1	1		1			77	
	Lucena	24	31	30	36							120	
	Malaga	132	128	53	64							403	
	Marbella	3	4	1	1	1	1	1	3			15	
	Motril	29	26	22	20	1	1	1	3			102	
	Ronda	31	36	36	25	6	10	6			1	163	
	Velez Malaga	73	60	49	49	7	6	4	4			256	
	Vera	23	71	16	14	2		2				82	
	Nijar	14	13	15	9			1	1			52	
	Alhabi la Real	14			5							49	
	Ronda	35	40	36	25	6		6			1	163	
	Velez Malaga	73	60	49	49	7	6	4	4			256	
	Vera	23	71	16	14	6		2				82	
	Nijar	14	13	15	16	6		1	1			82	
Jaen	Alcala la Real	14	10	4	5	2	1	2	1			49	372
	Andujar	3	4	3	1	1	1					27	
	Baeza	26	21	17	10	12	12	6	4		2	104	
	Jaen	12	13	9	7							26	
	Linares					1	1	1				20	
	Martos	4	2	1	1							13	
	Torredonjimeno					1	1					15	
	Ubeda	23	15	9	4	7	6	5				80	
Mancha	Alcaraz	2		2		1	1					6	74
	Almagro		2		1							12	
	Ciudad Real					4	3	3	7			17	
	Daimiel	2	2	1	2							8	
	Infantes	8	3									30	
	Manzanares		2		1							1	
Murcia	Carabaca					1	1					6	735
	Caravaca	18	12	8	8	10	2	5				81	
	Cieza	3	2			3	1					11	
	Mula	6	11	1	1						4	29	
	Lorca	66	50	25	31	4		1	1		1	135	
	Moratalla	5	3	2		1						16	
	Murcia	100	56	70	46	6	7	2	1		6	342	
	Segura de la Sierra	6	4								1	18	
	Segura	15	12	1	3			1				50	
	Tovarra					2	2					4	
	Villena	4	2									10	
Sevilla	Antequera	50	50	33	35	3	2				2	175	4084
	Cadiz	163	220	92	105	2	15	1			2	598	
	Carmona	17	18	8	6							50	
	Ecija	43	38	22	27						1	130	
	Fregenal											10	
	Gibraltar	15	13	11	10						1	50	
	Isla de Leon	34	43	20	12							103	
	Puerto de Santa Maria	52	53	28	37							167	
	Sanlucar de Barrameda	112	96	77	82							375	
	Sevilla	333	694	292	291	30	30	10	16	6	2	1716	
	Xerez											12	
	Xerez de la Frontera	211	274	121	112	3	3	1				674	
Segovia	Capital	1	4	1		1						7	7
Soria	Capital	2	6	2	6	6	6	4	1			33	33
Toledo	Alcala					1	2	1				100	257
	Alcazar de S. Juan	22	24	17	5	1	2			2			
	Corral de Almaguer		2	1		1	12	2	30			125	
	Ocaña	24	21	13	13	4		1					
	Talavera	1	2	2	1								
	Toledo	4		1								4	
Toro	Capital					3	1					4	4
Principado de Asturias	Oviedo	7	20	20	4					10	2	50	50
Poblaciones de Sierra Morena	Carolina												
Resumen General		2780	2793	1724	1692	384	301	211	112	83	24	8392	8392

census of all Gypsies in Spain. Two months after the passing of the Pragmatic signed by Charles III (September 1783), orders were sent out to all
corregidors to compile a detailed list of Gypsies domiciled in their
respective districts. These instructions were interpreted in such varied
ways that the Council was obliged to send out numerous memoranda and
eventually ended up with two series of lists, drawn up in 1784 and 1785,
which largely complement one another and together provide very precise
information on a total population of 12,090 Gypsies. This is how we
come to know the surnames, first names, ages and occupations of all
Gypsy heads of family residing in Spain at the time, as well as of their
wives, children and other family members under the same roof. Some of
these lists even give physical descriptions of the individuals concerned.

Region by region, Andalusia was home to the greatest proportion, regis-
tering over 67% of Spain's Gypsy population. Next was *el Levante* (the
central Mediterranean coastal region) with 14%, Catalonia (7.9%),
Estremadura (5.2%) and New Castile (3.3%). In Aragon, Old Castile and
Léon, the numbers drop below 1%. No Gypsies were registered in the
remaining provinces: Galicia, the Basque Provinces, and the Canaries.

The case of Andalusia

Within Andalusia itself, the Gypsy population was distributed as follows:
Cadiz had the highest proportion, with 16.5% of the Gypsy population of
the country as a whole, followed by Seville with 15%, Grenada (11.1%),
Malaga (9.1%), Almería (6.4%), Cordoba (4.1%), Jaén (3.8%) and
Huelva (1%). The information available from Andalusia also suggests
better than average integration of the Gypsy population: it is here that the
percentage of Gypsies working as blacksmiths – a trade expressly forbidden them by law, as we have seen, and a privilege reserved for those
deemed to be well-integrated – is highest (41%), while the proportion
engaged in the compulsory occupation of farming is lowest, at 23%.
Here, too, the highest proportion of mixed marriages was to be found
(7.3% of all couples in the Gypsy census), while they rarely amounted to
2% elsewhere in Spain.

The Andalusian miracle

This data establishes that Andalusia was unique with regard to the Gypsy
population there. The underlying reasons for this are diverse. Some are

historical: we know, for example, that there had once been a strong Moorish presence in the towns and villages and that the gaps created by their expulsion were filled by Gypsies. We know, too, that social coexistence with ethnic minorities engaged in certain reserved occupations was by no means alien to the tradition of openness and hospitality that characterised the region.

Among the economic factors contributing to Gypsy integration in Andalusia, we note the existence of *latifundia** which provided massive temporary employment through seasonal labour. Even more significantly, it was an agricultural society which had developed horse-trading in a particular way and accorded certain types of work, such as blacksmithing and itinerant trading, special prestige. Thus Gypsy specialisations found a favourable terrain in Andalusia.

Flamenco: a philosophy and a way of life

We cannot overlook the hidden affinities between the Gypsies and the Andalusians, two peoples who are different but nonetheless share a number of values and traits: generosity, hospitality, a strong religious bent (or should we say a form of paganism?), the cult of honour, of courage, in short of a certain *machismo*, an ability to live in the present and, of course, a love of celebration. These shared characteristics facilitated what we might call Gypsy-Andalusian 'osmosis' and gave rise to a 'flamenco philosophy'. The word *flamenco* – which as we have seen originally referred exclusively to the Gypsies themselves – covers not only the musical art shared (and sometimes fiercely contested) by both the Andalusian and the Gypsy communities, but also refers to a way of life, a set of attitudes, chief among which are prodigality, a hair-trigger temper, insane passion and a contempt for 'polite behaviour' and material values. According to a famous saying, *los Flamencos no comen* ('flamenco aficionados do not eat'), and it is true that the search for extraordinary moments of communication and quasi-mystical musical exaltation in the course of intimate gatherings known as *juergas** has nothing whatever to do with the satisfaction of 'vulgar' appetite, despite the fact that consumption of alcohol (in the form of *fino*, the heady wine of Jerez) is a powerful stimulant of the *cante** in this bid to transcend our 'normal' physical limitations.

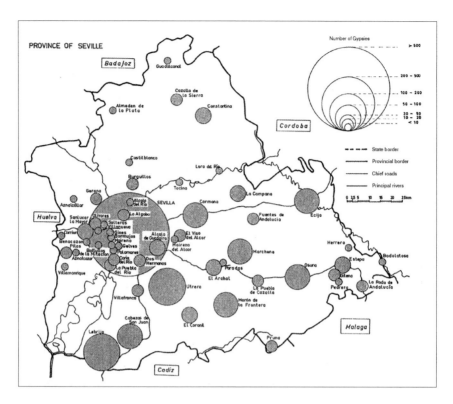

Map showing geographical
distribution of Gypsies in
the province of Seville

The geographical framework

At the end of the eighteenth century 'Gypsy Andalusia' was not the whole of the province, and 'Flemish' families were very unevenly distributed within it. In fact the two regions of Cadiz and Seville accounted for nearly half (46.8%) of the Gypsies in Andalusia, with 16.5% in Grenada, 13.5% in Malaga, Almería and Jaén each under 10%, and a mere 1.6% in Huelva, the least Gypsy region of Andalusia. Within Cadiz and Seville, sixteen localities stand in sharp contrast to the area as a whole, with some 821 Gypsy families, nearly a quarter of the entire Spanish Gypsy population at the time. These towns were, in order, Seville, Jerez, Cadiz, Arcos, Sanlúcar, Puerto de Santa María, Lebrija, Utrera, San Fernando (*La Isla*), Puerto Real, Ecija, Marchena, Medina Sidonia, Morón, Osuna and Carmona. All of these towns are considered flamenco strongholds, and most of them are part of what is known as the 'cradle', that special zone where the *cante* first appeared before spreading throughout Andalusia and spilling over its borders.

The great flamenco family

The largest Gypsy families were: Vargas, Jiménez, García, Reyes, Monje, Heredia, Fernández, Moreno, Flores, Cruz, Montoya, Bermúdez, Cortés and Peña. Other families noted were (in alphabetical order): the Carrascos (blacksmiths in Puerto de Santa María, agricultural labourers and sheep-shearers in Lebrija), the Espletas (butchers in Sanlúcar de Barrameda), the Junqueras (concentrated mostly around Arcos), the Loretos (field labourers at Lebrija), the Nuñez (blacksmiths at Cadiz, Puerto de Santa María and Ecija, farmers in Jerez and mule-drivers in Morón), the Ortegas (blacksmiths in Puerto Real), the Pavóns (blacksmiths in Castilblanco), the de los Santos (sheep-shearers and blacksmiths in Seville, and blacksmiths in Puerto Real), the Sotos (sailors and blacksmiths at Cadiz, but also numerous at Malaga), the Torres (butchers, field labourers and sheep-shearers at Utrera, and weavers at Marchena), and the Valencias (merchants and sheep-shearers at Ecija, masons at Jerez and at Sanlúcar de Barrameda).

These are the great names of flamenco, and nearly all twenty-five of these families are related: in the eighteenth century, as in the present day, these same names appear again and again in the marriage records, with the result that the singers of today are all part of one great flamenco family. In fact they are all cousins, and intermarriage has given rise to numerous instances of double surnames such as Peña Peña, Soto Soto, Vargas Vargas and so on.

Instances of people having ths same name abound, but Gypsies tend to go by nicknames (*motes*) which sometimes become hereditary (*apodos*) and may be transformed as required into artists' soubriquets. The great majority have achieved fame under these nicknames: *El Fillo* (Francisco Ortega Vargas), *Manuel Torre* (Manuel de Soto Loreto), *La Sarneta* (Merced Fernández Vargas), *Curro Frijones* (Francisco Antonio Vargas), *Curro Durse* (Francisco Fernández Boigas), *El Pinini* (Fernando Peña Soto), *Joaquín El de La Paula* (José Fernández Torres), *Manolo Caracol* (Manuel Ortega Juárez), *Terremoto* (Fernando Fernández Monje), *Antonio Mairena* (Antonio Cruz García), *El Sordera* (Manuel Soto Monje), *El Mellizo* (Enrique Jiménez Fernández), *Manolito El de María* (Manuel Fernández Cruz), *Paco la Luz* (Francisco Valencia), *Parrilla de Jerez* (Manuel Fernández Molina), *El Chozas* (Juan José Vargas Vargas), *El Chocolate* (Antonio Nuñez Montoya), *El Agujeta* (Manuel de los Santos), *Manuel Morao* (Manuel Moreno Jiménez), son of *El Morao* (Manuel

Moreno de Soto y Monje), *José Mercé* (José Soto Soto), *Camarón de la Isla* (José Monje Cruz), among so many others. This brief list already reveals many family links: an inextricably tangled genealogical skein.

These Gypsy-Andalusian families, doubly 'flamenco' (in the literal sense of 'Flemish' [that is, Gypsy, as already discussed], and as the stock whence flamenco artists spring), should serve to put an end to the interminable squabbles – usually of a racist bent – which persistently rock the little world of flamenco. The existence of these families and their enormous contribution to the art are difficult to dispute. Their members include not only a good number of the great interpreters of the present day, but also the majority of the best creative talents of the past. Moreover, the fact that they comprise a numerically small, geographically limited group should convince even the most intransigent of the anti-Gypsy lobby.

At the outset, then, it was not Spanish Gypsies in general who were involved in the flamenco phenomenon, although it has subsequently tended to spread throughout a very large proportion of the Gypsy community, for whom it has become a sort of ethnic music. 'Andalusianists' point out, not without justification, that there are Gypsies all over the world, but that flamenco appeared only in Andalusia. We could go further: only in a small part of Andalusia, limited to the lower valley of the Guadalquivir, with two eastward extensions towards Cadiz and Morón. We can also emphasise that, initially, flamenco was not a generally Andalusian phenomenon either, although it has demonstrated – indeed, continues to demonstrate – extraordinary powers of diffusion. Flamenco is now an essentially Andalusian phenomenon, but this is not to say that all Andalusians accept it or identify with it – far from it. Once again, we are dealing with a family affair, and if the flamenco family today has branches all over the planet, it is nonetheless a single, great family.

The obscure origins of flamenco art

What came to pass within these few Gypsy-Andalusian families, capriciously dubbed *Flamencos* because some of them possessed service records and Privileges attesting to outstanding service in the Flemish campaigns, these families so convolutedly interwoven that in the end they constitute a single entity? To understand this we must go back to the ancient folklore and popular music of which Gypsies were, for so long, the main and almost the exclusive professional performers. We must also consider the slow cultural osmosis which occurred in those localities where, thanks to their various activities, these families were perfectly integrated. We are dealing, in fact, with an instance of acculturation or, more precisely, of *transculturation*, since the successful merger of two musical cultures, the Gypsy and the Andalusian, gave rise to a third, utterly novel form: flamenco. Andalusia is not, as we know, the only place where such a process occurred, but the incomparable character of flamenco is almost certainly due to the extraordinary richness of the Andalusian heritage and the fact that it has a far greater affinity with the Oriental traditions of the Gypsy people than is the case in other Western countries.

Gypsies' professional music

To begin with, the Gypsies contented themselves with reproducing, as faithfully as possible, local styles for a local audience. Needless to say, this fidelity did not preclude a certain adaptation to the musical conventions and interpretation characteristic (to some degree) of Gypsies all over the world. Any music heard and reproduced by a Gypsy performer instantly acquires a distinctive tone, a 'colouring': it is somehow 'Gypsified'.

Gypsy dancer near Seville

This is how traditional Spanish song styles like the *seguidilla*, the *villancico* (Christmas carol) and the *romance* (ballad) gradually acquired the qualifying adjective 'Gypsy'. When these styles, corresponding to the repertoire habitually performed by Gypsies in the streets and marketplaces during local festivals, came to be adapted for the theatre, the staging instructions nearly always specified that they are to be interpreted 'in the Gypsy manner'. This tells us that *Payo* imitations of 'Gypsy' or 'pseudo-Gypsy' music and dance go back a long, long way.

Gypsy ballads

Gypsies were also to play an important role in the conservation of musical genres which would otherwise have died out. Ever quick to take on the latest musical fashion and remodel it in their own style, their loyalty to tradition was equally strong. A nineteenth century observer, Estébanez Calderón, mentions them as the last remaining performers of the very ancient *zarabanda*. As the ballad-sheets once hawked from village to village by blind pedlars gradually disappeared, the Gypsies were to preserve their precious contents, using them only when celebrating amongst themselves, or to lull their babies to sleep: Pepe, brother of the great *cantaor** Manuel Torre, remembered hearing their grandfather singing the ballads *Bernardo del Carpio* and *Gerineldo* as *nanas** (lullabies). The length and somewhat monotonous style of these ancient songs lent them naturally to this adaptation. Dolores Juárez de la O, better known as *Dolores La del Cepillo*, a Gypsy from Puerto de Santa María, took the central portion from a famous ballad, *Las hermanas reina y cautiva* (The Sisters Queen and Captive) – which is in effect a lullaby within the song's narrative – to transform it into a true *nana:*

> Ea, ea, la ea...
> Hija mía de mi alma
> y también del almita mía,
> que si te cogiera yo a ti en España
> que yo a ti te cristianaría
> y por nombre te pusiera
> que y Anita de Alejandría,
> que así se llamaba tu mare
> y una tiíta que a ti te mecía...
> (included in *Magna Antología del Cante Flamenco*, Hispavox, S/C. 66.201)

Sleep, my baby, sleep...
My daughter of my heart
And of my little soul too,
If I could bring you with me to Spain
I would make a Christian of you
And I would give you as your name
Anita of Alexandria,
For that was your mother's name
And the name of the auntie who rocked you to sleep...

The use of *romances* in family celebrations, and in particular at Gypsy weddings, is equally evident in the following version of an *alboreá* (wedding song), sung by Manuel de los Santos Gallardo (*Agujeta el Viejo*), in which scraps of *romances fronterizos* (ballads about relations with the Moors at the time of the reconquest of Spain) intermingle with traditional Gypsy wedding themes (here, the bride's crown and the formula generally employed to evoke the satisfaction felt by her father):

El rey moro con la paz
¡qué bien ha queao!
toíta tu gente t'han coronao,
pues dile que entre, se calentará
porque en esta tierra no hay cariá.

The Moorish king with peace
How lucky he is!
Your whole family has crowned him.
Well, tell him to come in; let him warm himself
For in this country there is no charity.

Of course, the *romances* have not been preserved by Gypsies alone. An audio anthology edited by José Manuel Gil under the title *Romancero Panhispánico* (1992) brings together a hundred or so, collected from the various regions of Spain as well as from Sephardic communities throughout the world. It is interesting to observe how these different versions, nearly all of them sung, are influenced by the musical styles of the regions in which they are performed. Among the Eastern Jews, Greek and Turkish influences are very apparent, while in the Castilian regions the melody is rudimentary, often close to recitation – but Gypsy versions stand out from all others in their typically flamenco approach. This should not surprise us, but if we carefully compare two versions of a single traditional *romance*, one collected from the *Payo* (non-Gypsy) oral tradition, the other among Gypsies, we instantly remark the characteristic traits with which the latter have, quite unconsciously, transformed the original melody. In fact what we can observe is the genesis of a new genre arising from interpretative distortion of the old.

This experiment is significant in more ways than one, for the *romance*, part of the Gypsy repertoire since the sixteenth century, is today considered the oldest of the flamenco song styles. Its features, and in particular its length, have prevented its commercialisation, confining it – as we have seen – to private occasions. Thanks to these circumstances, it has evolved very little – at any rate far less than the other flamenco *palos* (styles) – and it gives us a window onto the most archaic stages of the *cante*. The *romances* appear to be the source of the *tonás**, those supremely original unaccompanied songs from which almost all the others probably derive.

The Seguiriya*

The knottiest problem is posed by the *seguiriya* (or *siguiriya*), whose name is simply the Gypsy-Andalusian pronunciation of *seguidilla*, mentioned above, as it already figured in the Gypsy professional repertoire as far back as the seventeenth century, and perhaps even earlier. The *seguidilla* is probably among the most ancient of the sung dances of the Iberian peninsula, because stanzas constructed in the same form – four alternate lines of seven and five syllables, perhaps followed by a tercet – are also to be found in the *Mozarabic* kharjas** (or *jarchas**) which sometimes terminate *muwashshah**, Arabo-Andalusian poems dating back to the eleventh century. Its longevity is astonishing, for it continues to stir the passions even today in the form of the *Sevillanas*, Seville-style *seguidillas* which have spread throughout Spain and beyond.

The *seguiriya*, as it is usually written, takes both its name and its metric form from the *seguidilla*. The only difference is that the third line (of quatrains) or the second (of tercets) has eleven or twelve syllables instead of seven, as if a supplementary five-syllable line had been appended. These literary comparisons lose much of their relevance when we note that the sung *copla* (stanza) bears only a distant relation to the written, poetic form. An example will illustrate the point. Here is a classic *seguiriya* in its conventional written form:

> Una noche oscurita
> a eso de las dos
> la daba voces a la mare de mi alma
> no me respondió.
>
> *Darkest night*
> *Two in the morning*
> *I cried out to my darling mother*
> *There was no reply.*

Here, by contrast, is how Pastora Pavón, known as *Niña de los Peines*, interpreted this *copla*, with great gaps in the vocal filled by the guitar, heaving sighs, abrupt stops (sometimes right in the middle of a word) and numerous melismata (melodic prolongations of the sung vowel, here indicated by an accent):

aaáĭ	
....	Le dábá vocés
aaa-í-i-i, una noché oscuritá	....
....	le daba voces a la mare dé mi arma, nó/
á eso de/	ó me re/
e las dos	espondió.
a esó dê las dós, á eso de/	Voces le daba a mi mare dé mi arma dé/
e las dós.	mi co/
....	orazón.

Clearly this sung version is no longer susceptible to literary analysis, for its strophic divisions, entirely determined by the rhythm of the melody and the performer's breath control, no longer correspond to the meaning of the words. The metre and the words themselves explode, swept away in a shattering wail broken with sobs. In effect an inexplicable gulf has formed between the *seguidilla*, as light and carefree in its musical form as in its lyrics, and the sublime, dramatic, heart-rending *seguiriya*.

At the close of the eighteenth century a foreign visitor, Henry Swinburne, noted that the Gypsies of Spain still danced and sang the joyful traditional *seguidillas*:

> Both sexes are equally skilled at the dance, and they sing *seguidillas*
> in a manner gay or tender that is particular to them.

Not long afterwards, flamenco was to spring up abruptly among the Gypsy families of Lower Andalusia. One of the jewels of this sombre and

'Gypsi'

tormented art was to be the *seguiriya*, of which Ricardo Molina very aptly says:

> The seguiriya is the cry of a man mortally wounded by destiny. It can express only profound emotion, radical affliction, the tragedy of the human condition.

So what occurred in the time between these two quotations? The name has not changed, or at any rate not much, nor has the metric form – but the melody and lyrical genre are utterly transformed. The *seguidilla* is a gay and carefree ditty to accompany the dance. Its themes, melodies and accompaniment to a three-beat measure are typical of Spanish folklore. There is nothing surprising about this: musical styles of this sort are always present in folklore, and the Gypsies of long ago interpreted them in response to the demands of their local audience. The *seguidilla* was part of their professional activities, nothing more.

The Gypsy Ethos

The transformation worked upon the traditional *seguidilla* was singular indeed. The light air became 'deep song', a shriek straight from the gut, tinged with the bitter taste of blood. The fate – nearly always tragic, as we have seen – of the Gypsy community, its sufferings and atavistic anguish, here find direct expression. The Gypsy singer/guitarist Pedro Peña once said:

> You know how to express the song when you're carrying the pain of centuries with you. The Gypsy who knows how to do this gets it from his ancestors ... These are real experiences which have accumulated within him ... He suffers them; he lives them; he remembers all his own.

The traditional melody – very measured, very syllabic, in a word, very Western – of the *seguidilla* has mysteriously mutated into a long Eastern chant without limit or measure, with no break between tones, with a great unity of breath and silences. The poet Lorca describes it thus:

> Listen, my son, to the silence.
> It is a rippled silence,
> a silence
> where echoes and valleys glide
> and which turns faces
> towards the earth.

Finally, in place of the three-beat measure of the waltz, the fandango, or the *seguidilla*, the guitar accompaniment unfolds in twelve-beat rhythmic sequences comparable to those of Indian *ràgas*. All the ingredients of Oriental modal music are brought together here, including that singular correspondence known as the *ethos* or *modal sentiment* which links each style with a particular time of day or emotion. This is how Pedro Peña describes it, instinctively, without making reference to other musical cultures:

> The *soleá* is the song from midnight to one in the morning, when you feel good, when your spirit is still calm and the tears aren't yet brimming at the corners of your eyes. The *soleá* is for feeling fine! The *seguiriya*, by contrast, is for two or three in the morning. Your pain is right up at the surface, you've got to lance it. It's a confession. The *tonás* and the *martinetes** are for the dawn, and they crown the lot: they give you goosebumps and make your hair stand on end!

We have shown that the *seguidilla* and the *seguiriya* have nothing whatever in common except the similarity of their names. What we are dealing with here is in fact a different musical universe. The Gypsies wholly transformed the traditional ditty to reinvent it as a music forged in their own image, for themselves.

How did this process take place? Under draconian laws, as we have seen, these families were forced to renounce their language, costume, and virtually everything that made up their culture. The 1663 law even targeted music and dance – but it is very difficult to keep a Gypsy from singing for himself and those close to him, in his own home, particularly if he does so in the language of the majority, which will soon also become his own. Let us bear in mind that these *'Flamenco'* families, so well integrated into their Andalusian villages, sent their children to school and their women to Mass, paid their taxes, and dressed and talked like everyone else... but they did not have to sing like everyone else! The musicologist A. Larrea Palacín has suggested that, while language is constantly evolving, melodies may survive almost intact over millennia, and that this may give rise to divergence between words and music. Thus he explains the tendency of flamenco song, observed above in Niña de los Peines' interpretation of a *seguiriya*, to destroy the logical order of the text and break the metrical structure of the stanza.

Another hypothesis suggests an alternative explanation for this phenomenon. In this case we need no longer imagine a lengthy process of evolution, but a transformation realised in a relatively short period of time: the acculturation of an oppressed minority. A community may be dispossessed of its original culture in the space of a couple of genera-tions, as the Gypsies, among many other groups, amply prove. By con-trast, musical expression – rooted in the blood, the Gypsies would tell us – is far more difficult to eradicate. In practice what happens when a Gypsy sings verses borrowed from a culture other than his own and in a language imposed by law, but with an ear and ancestral melodies carried with him from the Orient, is the encounter of two incompatible cultural forms, resulting in a sort of explosion.

How to reconcile these diametrically opposed musical traditions? – one in which the melody is slavishly dependent on a text which is in turn imprisoned in a rigorously codified metrical mould, the other where the voice, while bound by other codes, seems as free as a breath of wind, and where the text is fragmented and dissolved in Eastern melismata. How the Gypsies have brought this about forms part of the sorrowful tale of their acculturation: they have unconsciously reconciled the irreconcil-able in a song-form born of the harsh encounter of East and West on Andalusian soil.

The *Vlax* Rom of Hungary

The musical styles of the Gypsies of Hungary offer intriguing analogies to what happened in Andalusia. At first glance the situation on the banks of the Danube appears less complex than that in the valley of the Guadalquivir. Professional Gypsy musicians there (who, as we saw in Chapter I, perform a range of hybrid styles all classed as *'Gypsy'*) belong to the group called *Romungro* (Hungarian Gypsy) who have been estab-lished in the country since the fifteenth century. They were forcibly set-tled under conditions very similar to those imposed on their cousins in Spain, and speak Hungarian as their usual language. Gypsies of the second group, whom the Hungarians call *Kolompar* or *Vlax* (Wallachian), arrived more recently from Romania; they may be nomadic, or semi-nomadic, and they usually sing in the Gypsy language (*Romani*). Their music, performed solely within the group itself, is limited to two genres. Firstly, there is song proper, known as *loki gili* or *loki djili* ('slow song'), within which two categories are distinguishable: short lyric stanzas simi-lar to Andalusian *coplas*, and narrative ballads comparable to the *romances.* Secondly, there is music to accompany the dance: *k'elimaski gili**, almost purely vocal but usually wordless, characterised by a rhythmic

use of the voice, termed *bögö** or *szaj bögö**. This strange technique, not unlike the use of *bol* syllables in the *tála* (rhythmic part) of Indian *dhrupad* music, provides a link with certain *jaleo* techniques, the distinctive cries uttered in highly rhythmic sequences to accompany flamenco dancing. Formerly the preserve of festivities within the *Vlax* Rom community itself, these styles have been adapted and launched on the international scene by Hungarian groups like *Kalyi Jag* and *Ando Drom*.

The *loki gili*, which may be considered as a sort of Oriental 'long song', has long intrigued those Hungarian musicologists who have devoted their attentions to it. Hungarian interest in traditional Gypsy music styles, alien to their own folklore yet often in symbiosis with it, goes back to Liszt and Bartók. Nearer to our own times, in the 1950s, a team of musicologists comprising Kamill Erdös, André Hajdu and József Vekerdi, began the task of isolating the original – *non-European* – characteristics of this music. Obviously such research was likely to highlight traits possibly shared with flamenco.

Since both *loki gili* and flamenco are forms rooted in Oriental music, they have quite a number of traits in common. It seems logical to begin by eliminating those shared with surrounding musical styles and which cannot, therefore, be assigned with precision to any single one of them. Hajdu identified monodic conception, a predominance of free rhythm (called *rubato* by European musicians), a general descending tendency in the melodic line, and the modal aspect as broad characteristics shared by all these music styles of Oriental origin.

Everyone who has studied the 'slow song' (*loki gili*) of the Hungarian Rom in detail has been struck by the same peculiarities: the fact that, in lyric song, the stanzas do not constitute a logical sequence with regard to meaning (which is equally true in the *coplas* of flamenco song), and the fundamental severance of melody and lyrics (as observed above with regard to the *seguiriya*). In order to break the metric structure of the stanza – which, as in flamenco, is often a quatrain of short (octosyllabic, sometimes hexasyllabic) lines – the Rom use various forms of 'padding': extra syllables, interjections, a range of exclamations at the beginning and/or end of lines, as well as the strange and most remarkable device of breaking off in the middle of a word, particularly in the penultimate syllable of the final line of each stanza, where they are accompanied by a very characteristic melodic formula in the finale.

Musicologists insist that these particularities are not to be found in any form of Central European music except Gypsy singing. We therefore appear to be dealing with unique characteristics, definitive ones, a sort of signature which enables us to identify and authenticate this music.

(Curiously, we are currently witnessing signs of interference between the musical styles of the *Vlax* Rom, for private use, and the professional, so-called *Gypsy* music traditionally performed by the *Romungro* group. Thus, for example, vocal rhythms of the *bögö* type have been introduced into instrumental *csardas* music and, above all, we observe that popular song in the so-called *Gypsy* style, sung in Hungarian, is rigorously modelled on the melodic schema of the *loki gili*, with its characteristic pause on the penultimate syllable and its formulaic finale.)

The Gypsy signature

These singular traits characterising the music of the Gypsies of Hungary are also to be found – in equal isolation from surrounding musical convention – in the purest and most archaic song styles of the flamenco repertoire: the *tonás*, some *seguiriyas*, and 'primitive' *soleares**, where the final break-off is often anticipated on the second or even third syllable before the last. With the exception of certain *alboreás* (wedding songs) of the Cadiz region, these traits are to be found neither in other flamenco song styles, nor in Andalusian folk music. Thus music styles as geographically distant and at first glance as different as the *loki gili* of Hungary and the *toná* of Andalusia manifest extremely tantalising structural analogies. A written example does not convey this as strikingly as actually listening to the music would do, but may give some idea of the phenomenon:

(a) Loki gili (performed by Mihaly Varadi, Kotaj village)

	Rat'enca na só/vav	
o ke	*numa sa gindinav;*	ke jaj!
aj!	*sa pal odi gindij,*	jaj!
ke mama	*so gáno te kér/av?*	
	I cannot sleep the whole night long,	
oh!	*for I do nothing but think;*	kay, aïe!
aïe!	*I'm all the time thinking,*	aïe!
what, Mama,	*what am I going to do?*	

(b) Toná (debla performed by Antonio Mairena)

¡Ay!	*En el barrió/ de Triana,*	
	se escuchabá en alta vóz:	
	– Pena de la viá tiene	¡ay qué!
to	*aquel que sea Cá/ló.*	

Aïe!	*In the Triana barrio,*	
	A voice was loudly heard:	
	– They are condemned to death	aïe, kay!
all	*those who are Gypsy.*	

The 'padding' – which we have transcribed to the side of the lyrics proper – occurs at the beginning and end of the lines of each stanza or *copla*. It is most copious in the Romani version, but we note a number of similarities, for example *ke jaj!* (a) and *¡ay qué!* (b). In both instances the break-offs or pauses are situated in the first and final lines. In the latter case they appear almost systematically in one of the final syllables; in both cases, the pause is followed by a reprise of the preceding vowel and of the same melodic formula in the finale. These can be transcribed as follows:

(a) ké/../erav
(b) Cá/../aló

The anti-Gypsy polemic

These technical details may appear insignificant. In fact their rarity, or, more properly speaking, their total absence from the surrounding musical environments of both the *loki gili* and flamenco, and the extreme precision of the traits shared by the two genres, makes them much more than simple coincidences. In the climate of intolerance, even of racial hatred, which regularly divides the flamenco world, they take on a symbolic significance. It is current conventional wisdom to assert – contrary to all the evidence – that the Gypsies had nothing whatever to do with the creation of flamenco; this is the line taken by self-styled 'Andalusianists', who think they insult their opponents by dubbing them 'Gypsyists'. The very terms are misleading, since the Gypsy families in question are also – as we have seen – Andalusian, sometimes more so than their detractors. Didn't Lorca explain that he chose to christen his celebrated *Romancero* as Gypsy, precisely because, for him, the Gypsy was the most representative constituent of Andalusia?

The book as a whole, though entitled 'Gypsy', is the Gypsy sheep-shearers poem of Andalusia. I have called it Gypsy because the Gypsy epitomises the loftiest, the most profound, the most aristocratic characteristics of my country; he is the most representative of its way of living, the keeper of the flame, the blood, and the alphabet of a truth both Andalusian and universal.

While it is legitimate for non-Gypsy Andalusians to lay equal claim to flamenco with the Gypsy-Andalusian community, there is little to be proud of in asserting that Gypsies cannot have contributed to its formation on account of their limited creativity, absence of poetic ability and so on.

The argument is nearly as old as the flamenco genre itself, but it took on a particularly dogmatic tone from the 1950s onwards, in particular with the declaration of Tomás Andrade da Silva, Professor at the Royal Conservatory of Music, Madrid, on the occasion of the launch, in 1954, of the first *Anthology of Flamenco Song*:

> There are no longer grounds for attributing a gypsy origin to the basic songs of flamenco: it has now been established that, with a few insignificant exceptions, the gypsies have never done anything more – although, when all is said and done, it is a great deal – than to lend certain Andalusian airs

the stamp of their inimitable personality, by interpreting them with a genius so authentic that we can well speak of a process of re-creation.

The phrase *'it has now been established that…'* is worth underlining, since it is presented as proof in and of itself, with no reference to evidence of any kind and no basis save the personal convictions of the author. One could compile a fair-sized book just by sticking assertions of this sort end to end – assertions which, despite their perpetrators' academic qualifications, demonstrate nothing but their basic ignorance of the facts.

Others were to go further, putting forward the equation: *Gypsies steal chickens* = *Gypsies steal music*, denying Gypsies any contribution save their performance. It should be noted that the same controversies and arguments have been going the rounds in Hungary since the time of Liszt and Bartók, and that certain contemporary musicologists do not hesitate to assert not only that the Gypsies have never invented anything, but that they are, moreover, very mediocre musicians.

It is obvious that not all Gypsies, nor indeed all Andalusian Gypsies, are musical geniuses. It is equally clear that flamenco could only have come into being in Andalusia, and it would be absurd to expect to see it arising spontaneously in the suburbs of Vienna or Warsaw! On the other hand, there are now enough demonstrative arguments and formal musicological data available to easily refute those who claim, for example, that when the Gypsies arrived in Europe in the fifteenth century they possessed no musical tradition of their own at all, or that they are utterly incapable of artistic creativity.

It is evident that the majority of writers (among whom musicologists are a tiny minority) who have contributed to the enormous bibliography currently available on the subject of flamenco, have had little if any knowledge of Gypsy music elsewhere. Some of them have heard of the 'professional' music played in Central Europe, like the instrumental music played in Hungarian cabarets and known as 'Gypsy music', and which obviously has nothing in common with the vocal music of Andalusia, known as *flamenco*. None of them is aware of the existence of the private repertoire of non-professional Gypsy musicians, discussed above, whence their conviction that Gypsies in general are limited to imitating local musical styles, have no musical tradition of their own, and are consequently incapable of creativity in this field.

As we know, ignorance is at the root of all racial prejudice. It is ignorance which has given rise to diametrically opposed attitudes towards the

Gypsies: attraction and repulsion, fascination and hatred. It is ignorance that accuses them of having dissolute morals – a very revealing error for those familiar with the rigidity of their moral code – and that has charged them with every crime from the abduction of children to cannibalism. It is ignorance, too, which idealises and mythologises them until they come to be seen as the survivors of a lost paradise of natural harmony, *joie de vivre* and unbounded freedom. These contradictory myths have coexisted from the very start and survive to the present day. They mask reality to such a degree that our ignorance of a whole community living in our midst is perpetuated.

Gypsy Andalusia and *Payo** Andalusia

In the case of flamenco and Andalusia the problem is complex and cannot always be attributed to simple racism. At the heart of what we may call 'the cradle of flamenco', at Jerez de la Frontera and in the many little villages in this part of Lower Andalusia, the genre is essentially Gypsy, with a handful of exceptions. The most celebrated of these was Antonio Chacón, of unknown parentage but adopted by a *Payo* cobbler who bequeathed him his name and did his best to discourage a precocious talent for an art-form all too often disparaged because of its origins. Chacón's models were Gypsy artists such as Enrique 'El Mellizo' and Curro Durse, as well as another *Payo* of genius, Silverío Franconetti (b. 1839), whose overwhelming passion for the *cante*, which he first heard at a Gypsy forge in Morón, was also discouraged by his father, an Italian serving in the Spanish Army. Essentially, flamenco in, for example, Jerez is a Gypsy phenomenon, and a family affair. Virtually all of today's singers come from famous artistic 'dynasties' or can point to flamenco antecedents (professional or otherwise) as far back as the memory of their lineage goes. All claim that their art runs in their veins, that this is recognised by their fellow citizens, and that they have never encountered the slightest hint of racism in their own region.

Once we start to move away from this most favoured region of Gypsy song, we come across more and more *Payo* (non-Gypsy) performers, both amateur and professional, and, whether we travel in the direction of Huelva or of Malaga, the influence of Andalusian folkmusic becomes more and more pronounced, and the singing style is noticeably transformed. Between these two schools – the Gypsy one of Lower Andalusia and the *Payo* one around its periphery – there is sometimes a total

absence of mutual understanding, each vehemently insisting that it alone
gave birth to flamenco.

The origins debate

Most misunderstandings arise with regard to flamenco's origins and
antiquity. We know that this singular art first emerged as recently as the
nineteenth century; all the evidence agrees on this point, but that does not
stop some from asserting that it has been practised on Andalusian soil
from time immemorial. To give a concrete example, the birth of the Cadiz
*alegrías** can be dated with a fair degree of precision, since we know the
historical circumstances (the aftermath of the War of Independence,
1808-1814) under which the form arose, and even the names of its principal originators (all from the nineteenth century). In spite of this, some
have claimed that the celebrated dancers of Cadiz, praised by Martial and
Juvenal in the 1st century A.D., were performing to *alegrías*.

Research of this kind could go as far back as the inhabitants of the
Kingdom of Tarsis or Tartessus, located in the Guadalquivir region
between the twelfth and sixth centuries B.C., if successive invaders –
Phoenicians, Greeks and Carthaginians – had left us any details about
their music. It is more than likely that the Tartessians had some sort of
music of their own; one can even suppose that it would have been
exposed to Eastern influences and that some of these characteristics
would have become integral to Andalusian folk music – but nothing gives
us grounds for assuming that this bore any resemblance to present-day
flamenco.

Authors grappling with the question of the origins of flamenco do not
generally go quite so far back, but they have (quite naturally) made reference to most of the musical cultures present in Andalusia in the period for
which we have historical records: the Arabs, the Jews, even the Byzantines*. The Gypsies' role has been emphasised by some, minimised or
actively denied by others. As for the Africans – who were a very strong
presence in the region during the sixteenth and seventeenth centuries –
they are almost completely overlooked.

The Jewish theory

The theory of Jewish influence on flamenco music, put forward in 1930
by Medina Azara in the *Revista de Occidente*, was very effectively

refuted by Hipólito Rossy in his book *Teoría del Cante Jondo* (1966). The analogies Azara draws between certain Jewish religious songs and the *saetas** of Andalusian processions are entirely without foundation, since the examples cited are very modern creations, in particular the *saeta* of Manuel Centeno, adapted to the *seguiriya* model. Moreover all one need do is to listen to Sephardic songs, preserved up to the present day among the descendants of the Jews expelled from Spain in 1492 – and in particular their versions of *romances* – to observe that these have nothing whatever in common with flamenco.

The Byzantine theory

The Byzantine theory, formulated by the Catalan musician and musicologist Felip Pedrell and taken up by Manuel de Falla, seems to be based on a confusion between the Byzantine liturgy and the early Spanish rite known as the *Hispanic* or sometimes the *Mozarabic** liturgy. One way or another, this particular rite, abolished by Pope Gregory VI in the 11th century, was not reconstructed until Cardinal Jiménez de Cisneros took on the task some four hundred years later. When we take into account that the liturgy was written down in *neumes* – simple aides-mémoire to facilitate oral transmission – we have grounds for doubting the fidelity of the reconstruction, let alone the reservations one might have regarding the influence of such a rite on totally secular music that would not make an appearance until the nineteenth century. As for de Falla's 1922 reiteration of Pedrell's Byzantine references – this must be seen in context. What the great Andalusian musician was attempting to do was to persuade the Grenada authorities to finance the first ever *cante jondo** competition. What better way than by convincing them that this music, so reviled and vilified by the generation of 1898*, might be of noble origin and thus merit rehabilitation?

This line of thought was obviously also an attempt to explain the clearly Oriental traits of this Andalusian style, namely its modal, enharmonic character and its distinctive long, unmeasured singing. The Byzantine liturgy – derived from the Syrian modal system – might very well have something to do with it, but why not turn to the more obvious candidate? Arabic music was played on Andalusian soil for over seven hundred years.

Arabic music

On this particular point de Falla once again follows his mentor, Felip Pedrell, according to whom Spanish music owes nothing at all to the Arabs who, by contrast, were greatly influenced by Spain. In connection with this he mentions a number of points common to the so-called *Arabo-Andalusian** music of Morocco, Algeria, and Tunisia on the one hand, and to some folk and popular music styles in Andalusia itself on the other.

Without re-opening the whole debate, it is clear that musical influences in *Al Andalus* (Muslim Andalusia) operated in both directions. The Arabic poetic form known as *muwashshah* terminates in a refrain or couplet known as a *kharja* (in Spanish, *jarcha*), which was widely borrowed from indigenous folklore and written in a Romance language – Mozarabic – sprinkled with Arabic words. These *kharja* or *jarchas* offer eloquent testimony to the bilingualism of Muslim Andalusia and the musical exchanges that were commonplace there. It is difficult to imagine that the author/composers of these great poems made for singing – the *muwashshah* – could have borrowed the words of their final stanza – the *kharja* – without also taking the music on board.

One of the most vivid traces of this exchange between Arabic music and Andalusian folklore is still visible – and above all audible – today, when we compare an Arabo-Andalusian band from Morocco with a *panda de verdiales**, one of the little folk ensembles from Malaga province. The same elements are to be found in both: metallic percussion in the form of rattles or small cymbals, a type of drum known as *duff* in Arabic and as *pandero* or *adufe* in Spanish, lutes played by plucking the strings (*'ud* in Arabic, *laud* in Spanish), fiddles which in both cases have replaced an ancient bow instrument (known as *rebab* in Arabic, *rabel* in Spanish), not to mention the guitars on the Spanish side. In both cases the singing style is highly syllabic and very far removed from the long melismatic wail characteristic of flamenco.

Certainly, as we have seen, there are similarities between Andalusian and Arabic music, but these must logically be sought in the vestiges of the traditions that co-existed between the seventh and the fifteenth centuries: in other words, in the Arabo-Andalusian music of the Maghreb and in the most archaic folklore of Andalusia – the *verdiales**, for example. If, by contrast, later Arabic musical forms (which reached North Africa from Iran and Iraq via Egypt) and flamenco (which, it must be borne in mind, came into being in Lower Andalusia only in the nineteenth century) exhibit analogies *absent from Andalusian folklore*, some other factor must have intervened. Despite the precautions de Falla had to take in the course of his 1922 oratory before the Grenada authorities, he does not hesitate to identify Gypsies as the linking element:

> And it is these tribes, coming – according to the historical hypothesis – from the Orient, who in our opinion gave Andalusian song the new modality which constitutes the *cante jondo.*

de Falla's demonstration

In the same work from 1922, de Falla analyses, with great musicological precision, the shared traits of flamenco and Eastern music, in a long section entitled *Coincidences with the Primitive Song Forms of the Orient.* Here, curiously enough, there is no further reference to the Byzantines or Arabs (besides, the author has already given us both his own and Pedrell's opinion on this latter point), but only to *the Orient* and more precisely to *India.* Here is how he begins his exposition:

> The essential elements of the *cante jondo* exhibit the following analogies with some song forms of India and other peoples of the Orient.

A few lines further on de Falla repeats his allusion to 'primitive styles of India'. India, the Gypsies' place of origin, is thus his main focus, and the purpose of the exposé is to demonstrate, with a wealth of technological detail, Gypsy input into the development of the art form which he and Federico García Lorca call *cante jondo* and which we simply call flamenco. He develops the following five points:

> *Enharmony as a means of modulation.* This comprises the alteration of certain notes of the scale, and more generally the use of intervals of less than a semi-tone to modulate, that is, to pass from one key to another. In other words, de Falla is referring to the non-measurable aspect of the Eastern long chant as opposed to the tempered scale employed in the Occident.

> *We recognise as proper to the cante jondo the use of a melodic ambitus which rarely exceeds the limits of a sixth.* de Falla points out here that the sixth in question is not, of course, limited to the nine half-notes of the tempered scale.

> *The repeated, almost obsessive use of a single note, frequently accompanied by higher and lower appoggiatura.* de Falla adds that, thanks to this

process, all sense of metric rhythm disappears. We have already seen, in the example of the *seguiriya*, how the structure of a stanza of verse may dissolve into the melody.

While Gypsy melody, like primitive Oriental song styles, is rich in ornamentation, this is employed only at points where the emotive force of the lyric provokes expansion or exaltation.

The shouts used by our people to encourage or excite the dancers and guitarists have their origin in the custom still to be seen in similar circumstances among races of Oriental origin.

Current knowledge

Posterity took from de Falla only what it wanted to hear. It remembered the Byzantines and Arabs, and strove to relegate the Gypsy contribution to one of simple interpretation. The arguments outlined above were ignored or rejected out of hand, doubtless because they were too technical or simply too 'pro-Gypsy'. This is why, over the ensuing three quarters of a century, all published works on flamenco have covered the same old themes, repeated the same clichés, often reiterated the same errors, without troubling to critically examine or offer evidence in support of their basic hypotheses, which have been accepted as absolute truths.

The origins of flamenco seem likely to remain shrouded in mystery for some time to come, due to the circumstances surrounding its birth and musicologists' unwillingness to tackle the question. As long as the only efforts made in this field have as their sole aim the ruthless elimination of a given community from the competition, there is no chance of our knowledge progressing. The various points outlined in these pages merely take stock of our current knowledge. Yet, despite their limitations, they do enable us to identify the essential issues:

Neither the Byzantines nor the Jews had much to do with flamenco.

The issue of Arabic influences is far from resolved. A process of exchange between Arabic music and the popular music of Andalusia took place over more than seven centuries of Muslim presence in the region, and its legacy is still perceptible today in what remains of the primitive *muwashshah* (even after centuries of oral transmission), in music generally, and in that most authentic manifestation of Andalusian folklore, the *pandas de verdiales*.

It is in any case pointless to look for correspondences between an

Arabic music which, to all intents and purposes, died out in Spain over the course of the sixteenth century, and another musical style that came into being among the Gypsies of Lower Andalusia at least two centuries later. The exercise would be as absurd as seeking out Arabic etymologies for the word 'flamenco', which only came to designate this music during the nineteenth century.

Any trait common to both Arabic music and flamenco which is not also present in the most traditional forms of Andalusian folklore can only be explained by the intervention of other factors.

Among such factors the only plausible candidates are the Gypsies, whether they brought with them to Spain musical characteristics originating in India and in Iran (this latter being the source of Arabic music), as Manuel de Falla aims to demonstrate, or whether they found and adopted these traits *after* their arrival in Andalusia and kept them from dying out. In fact the most likely explanation seems to be that they reworked the vestiges of Andalusia's Oriental past on their own cultural loom. In any case, the appearance of a phenomenon as singular as flamenco – an island of Oriental music in a sea of Occidental culture – cannot be explained except by reference to active Gypsy participation, and against the background of an Andalusia eternally torn between two cultures. The Gypsy community, with its own particular genius and extraordinary facility for adaptation, finally brought these cultures into harmony.

Conclusion

T he present work is unlikely to put an end to the quarrels which have always divided the flamenco world. Its sole purpose has been to extricate the debate from a tangled skein of conflicting theories and put it back on track with the aid of a few basic historical facts and some musical observations. The initial period of flamenco's gestation and development was essentially Gypsy, whereas the second phase, which considerably expanded its repertoire and audience, was primarily *Payo* or Andalusian. The transmission within a number of Gypsy families of certain songs, and above all of a particular interpretative style and a way of *living* the flamenco, is incontestable fact, but this must not blind us to the role played by *Payo* artists of genius such as Silverío Franconetti (1839–1889), Antonio Chacón (1869–1929), Antonio Ortega, known as 'Juan Breva' (1844–1918), and so many other great names of flamenco without whom this art form, a minority phenomenon even in its own birthplace, would never have achieved the universal recognition it enjoys today. With the era of the 'singing cafés' (*cafés de cante*) which spanned the period from 1860–1910, flamenco changed both its range and its aesthetic. Voices were no longer inevitably raucous and broken; they soared towards the high notes with a timbre and tessitura more proper to arabesques and pure virtuosity than to the naked, unfettered expressivity of Gypsy song. The attraction of the *bel canto* was to be particularly strong during the so-called 'theatrical' period from 1910, when flamenco trod the boards and tried to compete with fashionable song. At the same time, the repertoire was enriched by taking on a good part of traditional Andalusian folklore, for example the great family of the *fandangos*, which were in turn to merge into the 'deep song' (*cante jondo*), thus giving birth to such gems as the *malagueñas, granaínas, tarantas,*

cartageneras and *mineras*. Other musical styles of Iberian origin, like the *farruca* and *garrotin*, or, from Latin America, *guajiras, milongas, vidalitas* and *rumbas* – were to attempt to integrate into the flamenco genre, with varying degrees of success. The most spectacular instance is that of the Afro-American *tangos*, which were all the rage in mid-nineteenth century Spain. The Gypsies were not slow to adapt these to their own particular sense of rhythm, so thoroughly indeed that these have become one of the noblest of styles, as authentically flamenco as the basic songs for which they are often mistaken.

Today, there are no real divisions within the flamenco genre. All the great *cantaores,* be they *Payo* or Gypsy, have the whole of the repertoire at their disposal, even though certain *cantes* are better suited to one type of voice or personality than another, and of course performers have their personal preferences. The osmosis has been so complete that there are Gypsies who can sing '*Payo* style' and *Payos* who 'sound Gypsy'. This is all to the good, just as it is legitimate for each side to insist on the originality, the excellence, indeed the primacy of its own style. What is less acceptable is the falsification of history to legitimise personal aesthetic preference. The obscurity of flamenco's origins has enabled any number of theories to proliferate; now it is time for serious research to provide some more reliable guidelines.

Gypsies assert that they get their basic styles through in-family transmission, and are usually able to cite forebears who – professionally or not – have been involved for three or four generations back. By contrast, as we have seen, the great *Payo* artists such as Silverío Franconetti and Antonio Chacón had to defy their fathers' wishes in order to embark on the flamenco adventure, and these individual vocations are rarely perpetuated in subsequent generations. These artists deserve no less credit than those born to the genre – quite the contrary, in fact – if we stop to consider that, Gypsy or not, with or without some element of atavism, achieving professional mastery of the flamenco art is always the fruit of a long, patient apprenticeship.

To put it briefly, the transmission of flamenco by traditional methods within certain Gypsy families is a perfectly verifiable fact. The matter is much more complex within Andalusian *Payo* circles, where flamenco and its transmission are not part of local folklore – very much alive in many regions, and too often misunderstood – and where the flamenco audience is a very minor section of the population. The relatively recent appearance of this musical genre in Andalusia allows us to reconstruct its history with a fair degree of accuracy and to take account of virtually all of its performers. These circumstances ought to suffice to dispel all speculation on the relationships between flamenco and the two communities concerned. The great creative artists of the genre are known, and if those associated with the so-called 'basic' styles like the *tonás*, *seguiriyas* and *soleares* are mostly Gypsies, the various forms of the *fandango* have tended to be linked with *Payo* names. Moreover, as we have seen, there is no point in searching the distant past for the origins of a genre that really did not come into being until the middle of the last century, and Andalusian folklore alone was in a position to directly receive the various influences detectable in, or claimed for, flamenco. We are also aware that in 1922 there was speculation which claimed more or less *mythical* origins for flamenco out of a desire to rehabilitate a genre totally rejected by the establishment. This speculation only served to fuel the quarrels that were to split the flamenco world over a common culture claimed by both *Payos* and Gypsies.

The international prestige acquired by flamenco over the course of the twentieth century resolved nothing, and the setting up of autonomous regions under the Spanish Constitution of 1978 rendered the problem even more complex. In effect Andalusia which, unlike Catalonia, the Basque Provinces, Galicia or Valencia, could not claim a distinct language of its own, focussed on flamenco as the symbol of its cultural difference. Yet the racist excesses which followed were not to issue from the Andalusian Flamenco Foundation, set up in Jerez in 1988 at the initiative of the Autonomous Assembly of Andalusia (*La Junta de Andalucía*), but rather from isolated Andalusianist circles, gravely wounded by what they deemed the excessive credit given to the Gypsies for a musical form which they considered their legitimate property. Far from sharing the views of Lorca, for whom the Gypsy epitomised Andalusia, they were infuriated to see the image of their homeland mixed up, both in the rest of Spain and abroad, with an oft-despised minority of foreign origin. Many Andalusians were deeply disturbed by the clichéd image, developed largely for tourists, which was imposed on them during the Franco regime: guitars, castanets and flounced costumes. Today, those Andalusians who identify with a flamenco culture (part of whose appeal is its supposed aristocratic pedigree) cannot reconcile this with seeing Gypsies in the limelight, and this is quite natural.

It is not, however, grounds for a declaration of war, nor for pointless attempts at falsifying historical and musicological facts. The data put forward in this study are all easily verifiable, and are not intended to form part of a polemic. If Gypsy participation in the development of flamenco is a demonstrable fact, this is not to dispossess Andalusia of something it holds dear. The second stage of flamenco history, during which folk *fandangos* were to be transformed into *deep songs*, is at least as important as the first: flamenco as we know it today is inconceivable without this process. We have also emphasised how the period leading up to the emergence of flamenco was one in which the Gypsy community assimilated indigenous music styles, and that it was thanks to this process that a new art form was born. Flamenco could not have come into being without the concurrence of all the factors described above, and it is precisely its Andalusian character which makes it unique among Oriental musical forms. Like all important cultural phenomena it was born of encounter, and all the components of this encounter – the people, of course, the Gypsy families and the Andalusians, but also the venue itself, the hospitable soil of Lower Andalusia – were indispensable to the process.

The fact that Andalusians have come to recognise themselves in 'Gypsy' music, once universally rejected, but which they have so taken to heart that they now dispute the ancestry of their *Caló** compatriots reveals a great deal about a collusion which has been going on for centuries, and which no one can really disavow. Through the songs they perform (especially those known as the 'basic' songs), the words they sing (often composed by celebrated Gypsy artists, studded with *Caló* [Gypsy dialect], and loaded with allusions to the 'Gypsy' way of living), and their constant reference to a 'flamenco' (which is to say a Gypsy-Andalusian) way of thinking and behaving, Andalusians identify with a hybrid culture they can well feel proud of. Another form of identification, no less significant, is the fact that at fiesta time young Andalusian women all dress up as *Flamencas* – that is, as Gypsies – donning the long, flounced, colourful spangled dresses worn by Gypsy women a century ago, when Gypsy horse-dealers still reigned over the great animal fairs of Andalusia. It is true that following a fashion or putting on a costume does not necessarily imply any degree of sympathy for those being imitated, and that carnival disguises are mostly a way of breaking taboos, but it is no less true that these Gypsy symbols, which Andalusians brandish like a banner, testify to a shared past perhaps less small-minded and richer in genuine values than the era in which we presently live. At a time when the *Payo* or *Gadjo* world is foundering in the cheerless anomie of uniformity and devising new ways to strip the Gypsies of the 'outmoded' values that they have succeeded in preserving right up to the present day (solidarity, family, a contempt for material wealth, a strong sense of celebration…), Andalusians cannot be the only ones to recognise the cultural debt we owe to a people too often dismissed as having 'no culture' and who can give us, with or without music, a few lessons in humanity.

Part Two

Two hundred Gitano flamenco artists

from the beginning of flamenco to the present

The following list is far from exhaustive. It has been limited to two hundred for purely practical reasons, but it should be noted that the additional names mentioned bring the total to nearer double that. In fact flamenco artists are so numerous that it is impossible to mention all of them; moreover, new ones are constantly appearing, not all of them within the borders of Spain itself. There are, therefore, grounds for lamenting the omission of certain important names. Among them are Ana 'La Alondra', 'La Andonda', Juan 'El de Alonso', Joaquín Amador Santiago, Antonia, Antonio, Leonor and María Amaya, Diego Amaya, 'Angustitas', Diego Antúnez, Carmen Heredia Bermúdez 'La Bali', Juan Barcelona, 'El Bengala', 'La Bizca', Pepa 'La Bochoca', 'Bochoque', 'El Boli', 'El Brujo', 'El Burriri', Enrique and Luisa Butrón, 'Tío Cabeza', 'Niño de las Cabezas', 'La Cachuchera', 'Ramón de Cadiz', 'Caganchín', Joaquín 'Cagancho', Juan Cortés 'El Cagón', 'Calderas de Salamanca', Juan Antonio Salazar 'El Camborio', Perico Campos, 'La Canastera', 'La Cantorala', Rafael 'El Carabinero', Enrique 'Caracol', Manuela 'La Caracola', 'Carapiera', Carlota, José Castellón, 'Tío Luis El Cautivo', 'La Chana', 'Charamusco', 'Chico Melchor', 'La Chicharrona', 'La Chirrina', 'Chocolate de Granada', 'El Cojo de Malaga', 'El Cojo Peroche', 'El Cojo Pavón', Rosario 'La del Colorao', 'El Cuervo', 'Tío Curro', 'Diamante Negro', 'Tío Diego El Picador', Ignacio Espeleta, 'El Faraón', 'La Faraona', 'La Farota', 'El Fati', 'La Feonga', Juan Feria, 'La Finito', Candelaria and Manuela Fernández, 'Tío Frasco', 'Tío Frascola', 'Tío Furgante', 'La Gallina', 'La Gamba', 'Gaspar', 'Gitanillo de Vélez', 'Tío José el Granaíno', 'Tío Gregorio', 'La Guaracha', José Iyanda, 'Isabelita de Jerez', Juan 'Jambre', 'La Josefa', 'El Juanata', Enrique Jiménez Espeleta 'Juanillo el Gitano', 'Tío Juanelo de Jerez', Soleá 'La de

Juanelo', Diego Fernández Flores 'El Lebrijano', 'La Lobata', 'La Loca' and 'El Loco' Mateo, 'El Loli', Ana and Antonio 'La Lora', Andrés 'El Loro', 'Tío Juan' and 'Tío Vicente' Maccarón, 'Tío Perico Mariano', 'Tío Matelo', 'La Mejorana', Fernando Ortega 'El Mezcle', María 'La Mica', 'Las Mirris', 'El Mojigongo', Carlota, José, Rita and Rosario Ortega Morales, 'La Moreno', 'La Obispa', Mariquita Ortega, 'Paco el Gitano', 'Luis de Pacote', 'Palomo el Gitano', Alonso Pantoja, Enrique Pantoja Monje, 'Tío José' and Ramón de Paula, 'El Pavirri', Ana and María Peña Vargas, Miguel 'el de La Pepa', 'La Perla de Triana', Luis 'el de la Pica', 'El Pichirri', 'La Pillina', 'Tío Pipoño', 'La Pirula', 'El Pollo Rubio', 'La Pompi', Antonio 'El Porío', 'El Puli', 'Curro Puya', Jesús Heredia 'El Quemao', 'La Quinina', 'El Quino', Pepe Ríos Amaya, 'Tío Rivas', 'La Roezna', Victor Rojas Monje, 'Román el Granaíno', 'Tía Salvaora', Manuela 'La Serna', Félix 'de Sanlúcar', José Serrano, 'La Talegona', 'El Tati', 'Perico El Tito', 'El Tiznao', 'El Troni', 'Felipe de Triana', 'El Turronero', Gaspar and Pepa 'de Utrera', Juan de Vargas, Juan Vargas Gómez, 'El Viejo de La Isla' and many more, with a special mention for the young people of Jerez, a 'next generation' as pure as it is brilliant: María Monje, 'Chico Pacote', Macarena Moneo, Juan Junquera, Joaquín 'El Zambo', Carmen 'La Cantarota', Antonio 'El Monea', 'Chiqui', Melchora Ortega, Ana de los Reyes, and Luis 'de la Tota'.

We have, by contrast, included two artists who, while not pure Gitano, amply deserve inclusion by merit of the 'Gitaneity' of their art and lifestyle: **Lola Flores** and **'La Piriñaca'** whose names are preceded by a § symbol to draw attention to their particular status, and who are not counted among the two hundred.

All choice is arbitrary, but we have tried to provide a balanced overview by devoting significant space to promising new arrivals alongside the great masters of the past. Each artist is listed alphabetically under his/her stage name **in bold**, which is given in quotation marks if it is a nickname (be it individual or inherited), followed by a letter indicating the discipline in question (S = song; D = dance; G = guitar). This is followed by the individual's legal name in brackets, date of birth, place of birth (if not a major city this is followed by the name of the province in brackets), date and place of death where appropriate, a brief resumé of their career and a brief sketch of the defining characteristics of their artistic personality and/or specialties.

Certain trends emerge on even a superficial reading of this list. The first is the absolute domination of song over the other disciplines, which is only to be expected within traditional flamenco. One is also struck by the fact that most of these artists are related and that they comprise, in effect, a single extended family; it is for this reason that we have emphasised the kinship links that bind them. Finally, one cannot fail to remark the repeated references to a single town in Lower Andalusia, Jerez de la Frontera, which emerges as the great breeding-ground of flamenco artists down through the years.

Note that there may be some confusion regarding the proper spelling of stage names (e.g. **Periñaca/Piriñaca**), and indeed surnames (e.g. **La Serna/Lacherna, Pabón/Pavón**), passed on orally. Such ambiguity is commonplace in flamenco.

Terms explained in the glossary are asterisked when they first appear in this section.

'El Águila' –S– (José Ortega Feria), Cadiz nineteenth-twentieth century. Son of **'El Gordo Viejo'** and grandfather of **'Manolo Caracol'**. *Banderillero* by profession, and a great interpreter of the songs of Cadiz.

'El Agujetas', Manuel –S– (Manuel de los Santos Pastor), b. Jerez de la Frontera (Cadiz) 1939. Nickname inherited from his father, **'Agujetas el Viejo'** (1908-1976). Grandson of **Justito Pastor** and nephew of **Domingo 'Rubichi'**. Worked as a blacksmith up to 1970 when he made his first recording and went professional. Won the Jerez *Cátedra de Flamencología* national prize for *cante** in 1977. Has given numerous concerts in Spain, the United States, Mexico and France. Possesses an *afillá** voice and excels in performing the purest ancient styles, the *martinetes** and *siguiriyas**.

'Agujetas Hijo' –S– (Antonio de los Santos Bermúdez), b. Jerez de la Frontera (Cadiz) 1939. Son of the above, from whom he inherited his raw, authentic style. Won first prize in the National Prisoners' Music Competition in 1992, a year after his sister **Dolores 'Agujetas'** did so.

'Albaicín, Pepe' –S– (José Maldonado Maldonado), b. Grenada 1927. Made his début in Grenada at the age of fourteen, then joined Juanito Valderrama's group. In 1979 he directed the group *Aires del Sacromonte* and later took part in the show entitled *Los últimos de la fiesta*. Has recorded many of Lorca's poems on flamenco themes.

'El Almendro' –S– (Enrique Ortega Monje), Seville 1882–1959. Grandson of **'El Gordo Viejo'**, son of the *cantaor** **Manuel Ortega Feria**, brother of the dancers **Rafael** and **Carlota Ortega**. Also worked as a *banderillero*. He was an excellent singer of *soleares** and created a new type of *fandango** heavily influenced by the *soleá**.

Amador. Many Seville-based Gitano artists share this name, among them **Diego** and **Ramón Amador Moreno**, both guitarists, born in 1951 and 1955 respectively; **Raimundo** and **Rafael Amador Fernández**, also guitarists (the latter is also a singer), born in 1960 and 1961 respectively and co-founders of the group *Pata Negra* which also includes their younger brother **Diego 'El Churri'**; their cousin **Juan José Amador**, a *cantaor* who specialises in accompanying flamenco dance.

Amaya, Carmen –D– (Carmen Amaya Amaya), b. Barcelona 1913, d. Bagur (Barcelona) 1963. Daughter of the guitarist **'El Chino'**, made her début at the age of six in Barcelona's *Las Siete Puertas* restaurant, going on to perform at the *Palace* in Paris and the *Villa Rosa* in Madrid before undertaking tours of Latin America, 1937–1940. In 1941 she appeared in New York's Carnegie Hall with **'Sabicas'** on guitar, going on to Paris and to London, where she was congratulated by the Queen. Over the course of her career she appeared in over thirty films, among them *La hija de Juan Simón* (1935), *María la O* (1936), *El embrujo del fandango* (1940), *Pasión gitana* (1945) and *Los Tarantos* (1963). Her dance style was extremely personal, anti-academic, indescribable, a dazzling explosion of a mysterious, savage power. She remains inimitable.

'Amaya', Juana –D– (Juana Gómez García), b. Morón de la Frontera (Seville) 1968. Related to **Carmen Amaya** through her mother, whence her stage name. Won her first prize at the age of nine, took part in the Second Seville Biennial in 1982, and danced with **Mario Maya** before taking on the role of Carmen in **Salvador Távora**'s 1996 production.

Amaya, Dolores ('Doloretas La Pescaílla') –S, D– (Dolores Amaya Moreno), b. Barcelona 1938. A cousin of **Carmen Amaya** and **'La Chunga'**, mother of **'Toñi La Pescaílla'**. Following her début in Barcelona, performed in many *tablaos** in Madrid, particularly at the *Café de Chinitas*. Many foreign tours, to Canada, the United States, Japan, France, Great Britain etc. Her specialties are *bulerías**, *rumbas** and *tangos**.

Amaya, Remedios –S, D– (Remedios Amaya Vega), b. Seville 1962. Made her début in various *tablaos* in Seville before launching herself on the wave of flamenco-rock. Recorded *Me voy contigo* in 1997. One of the younger generation of artists endeavouring to reconcile a commercial career with more orthodox singing styles.

'Anilla La de Ronda' –S, G– (Ana Amaya Molina), Rondo (Malaga) 1855–1933. Sang, accompanying herself on guitar, in the *cafés cantantes** of Malaga. **Pastora 'Imperio'** gave her a flounced flamenco dress *(bata de cola)*, Queen Victoria Eugenia presented her with a Manila shawl, and Federico García Lorca mentioned her in his famous 1922 lecture on the *cante jondo**. In 1930, at the age of seventy-five, she was the star of 'Andalusian Week' at the Barcelona Exposition.

'Ansonini del Puerto' –S, D– (Manuel Bermúdez Junquera), b. Jerez de la Frontera (Cadiz) 1918, d. Seville 1983. Performed mainly in Madrid *tablaos* and festivals such as the *Gazpacho* in Morón. A specialist in the *bulerías* genre, renowned for his sense of *compás**.

 Antúnez, Fernanda and **Juana** –D– (Fernanda and Juana Antúnez Fernández) **Fernanda**, b. Jerez de la Frontera (Cadiz) 1866, d. Seville 1935; **Juana**, Jerez de la Frontera (Cadiz), 1871–1938. Stars of Seville's *cafés cantantes*.

'Bacán', Pedro –G– (Pedro Peña Peña), Lebrija (Seville) 1951–1997. Son of the singer **Bastián 'Bacán'** and great grandson of **'El Pinini'**. Winner of the 1980 Jerez *Cátedra* national prize for flamenco guitar; was invited to the musicology department of the University of Washington in 1983, subsequently undertaking a great many tours with his large family under the collective name of *Le Clan des Pinini*. His *Nuestra historia al sur* show was presented at the 1990 Seville Biennial. Recorded four CDs that year under the title *Noches gitanas en Lebrija* in collaboration with his family, his father **Bastián**, his sister **Inés**, his cousin **'Pepa de Benito'** and many others, leaving for posterity a unique monument to a fluid, inspired guitar style, and to warm, intimate, unpretentious flamenco in the pure Gitano tradition.

'Bacán', Inés –S– (Inés Peña Peña), b. Lebrija (Seville) 1952. Took to public performance relatively late, in her brother **Pedro 'Bacán'**'s shows, an effort to recreate the atmosphere of family music-making. Interprets the ancient Lebrija styles inherited from her great-aunt **María Peña** and **'Tío Benito de Pinini'** in a highly personal, emotional manner. Took part in the Seventh *Caja Madrid* Festival, 1999.

Batista, Andrés –G– (Andrés Batista Francisco), b. Barcelona 1936. Trained in both classical and flamenco styles, made his début in the *tablaos* of Barcelona before going on a two-year Asian tour with the dancer **Queti Clavijo**, followed by numerous trips abroad accompanying, among others, **Vicente Escudero, 'La Singla'**, and **Carmen Amaya**. Appeared in the film *Los Tarantos*, the score of which included some of his compositions. He opened an academy in Madrid, gives recitals and music courses in Spain and abroad and publishes manuals of guitar technique. Recorded a solo album, *Paisajes y trilogía*, in 1993. Winner of many awards, he has created his own distinct style characterised by gentleness and harmony.

'**Bernarda de Utrera'** –S– (Bernarda Jiménez Peña), b. Utrera (Seville) 1927. Cousin of the above and sister of **Fernanda**, whose career she has parallelled in *festero** counterpoint to the greatest singer of *soleares* of the late twentieth century. The two sisters won the Gold Medal of Andalusia in 1994.

'**El Biencasao'** –D– (José Cortés Moreno), b. Seville 1951. Married to **Angelita Vargas** and father of dancer '**Joselito'**, he and his wife have performed in the *tablaos* of Seville and Madrid as well as at festivals and at the 1982 and 1984 Seville Biennials. Famed for his *bulerías*.

'**El Bola'** –G– (Agustín Carbonell Serrano), b. Madrid 1967. Son of the singer '**Agustín Montoya'** and brother of dancer **José Serrano**. Apart from his concert performances, also provides accompaniment for dancer '**El Güito'** and singer **Morente**.

'**La Bolola'** –S– (Rafaela Montoya Dávila) Jerez de la Frontera (Cadiz), 1910(?)-1984(?). A cousin of '**Paulera Viejo'**, she revived a very personal style of *bulerías* which fascinated professionals such as **Antonio Mairena, 'La Paquera'** and '**Camarón'**.

'**El Boquerón'** –S– (José Diego María Santiago Camacho), b. Seville 1947. Performs in Madrid *tablaos* and has accompanied some of the great figures of the world of dance, among them **Manuela Carrasco** and **Angelita Vargas**. Gave recitals at the Third Seville Biennial and the Second *Cumbre Flamenca* in Madrid. Tends to adopt the singing style of '**Manolo Caracol'**, to which his voice is particularly suited.

'**Borrico, María'** –S– (María Fernández Piña), b. San Fernando (Cadiz), nineteenth century. Sister of '**El Viejo de La Isla'**, she created a *siguiriya* style reputed to be very difficult to perform.

'El Borrico' (**'Tío Borrico'**) –S– (Gregorio Manuel Fernández Vargas), Jerez de la Frontera (Cadiz) 1910–1983. Son of **'El Tati'**, father of **'María La Burra'**, nephew of **'Juanichi El Manijero'** and cousin of **'Tío Parilla'**. An unconventional *cantaor*, gifted with an *afillá* voice, brilliant interpreter of the pure Gitano styles of Jerez: *siguiriyas*, *soleares*, *tangos* and *bulerías*. His career, launched in 1967, was all too brief.

'La Burra', María –S– (María Fernández Flores), b. Jerez de la Frontera (Cadiz) 1931, d. Seville 1996. Daughter of **'Tío Borrico'**, she began her brief professional career only after the death of her father, from whom she inherited an extraordinary sense of rhythm and a dark, sorrowful voice.

'Cagancho, Tío Antonio' –S– (Antonio Rodríguez Moreno), Seville 1820-(?). A blacksmith at Triana, father of **Manuel 'Cagancho'** (Manuel Rodríguez García) born in the same town in 1846. Both have been credited with the invention of particular types of *siguiriya*. The one popularly known as *reniego*, formerly attributed to Manuel, is today recognised as his father's creation, while the *remedio*, once credited to Antonio, is now attributed to **'Frasco El Colorao'**.

'Camarón de La Isla' –S– (José Monje Cruz), b. San Fernando (Cadiz) 1950, d. Badalona (Barcelona) 1992. His stage name was given to him when still a child by **'Joseico'**, an uncle of his mother's, because his pale skin, fair hair and general air of fragility were reminiscent of a little grey shrimp (*camarón*). He worked in the family smithy from a very early age but dreamed of being a bullfighter, and it was in bullfighting circles that he began to sing before going on to perform in country inns, particularly the *Venta de Várgas*. At the age of sixteen he went professional with **Miguel de los Reyes'** group, later touring with **Dolores Vargas** and performing in Madrid's *Torres Bermejas tablao*. Made his first recording in 1968, accompanied by guitarists **Antonio Arenas** and **Manolo Heredia**, but in later years was habitually accompanied by **'Paco de Lucía'** and later by **'Tomatito'**. His rhythmic singing, catchy refrains and the combined peculiarities of his style, voice and personality quickly appealed to a young audience with broad musical tastes. His official discography includes twenty-one titles, among them *La leyenda del tiempo* (1979), inspired by the work of Lorca, and *Soy libre* (1989), on which he is accompanied by the Royal Philharmonic Orchestra. His battles with drugs and then with the lung cancer that eventually killed him made him a living legend haunted by destiny, revered both before and since his death by Gitano and Payo, young and old alike. His voice could be gentle and tender or express fierce bitterness; either way, his singing was a shattering cry torn between a raging will to live and utter despair.

'**La Camboria**' –D– (Carmen Salazar Vargas), Seville (?–?). Following her début in her native district, La Macarena, she performed in Seville theatres and began to tour, first in North Africa and eventually throughout Europe. In 1964 she replaced **Carmen Amaya** at the *Théâtre de l'Etoile* for a month. She also achieved notable success in London's *Scala* theatre with a show built around the poetry of Federico García Lorca. Her style, based on gesture, is a very personal one.

'**Canela de San Roque**' –S– (Alejandro Segovia Camacho), b. San Roque (Cadiz) 1947. From the same family as '**Jarrito**' and '**Perico Montoya**'. Won first prize in the Mairena del Alcor competition, 1983. Shows a preference for traditional and *jondo* styles, as exemplified in the *siguiriyas* of '**Paco La Luz**' and **Francisco 'La Perla'**.

'**Cantero**', **Juan** –S– (Juan Jiménez Salazar), b. Agudo (Ciudad Real) 1939. A singer who specialises in accompanying dancers, he is also a remarkable interpreter of the characteristic styles of Estremadura.

Cantoral, 'Tío' José –S– (José Cantoral). With **Juan** and **Manuel Cantoral**, early nineteenth century Jerez singers of legendary status. Almost nothing is known of them, save that **Manuel** sang *tonás**.

'**Caracol, Manolo**' –S– (Manuel Ortega Juárez), b. Seville 1909, d. Madrid 1973. A descendant and heir of numerous flamenco 'dynasties', including those of '**El Planeta**', **Enrique 'El Gordo Viejo'** and '**Curro Durse**'. Achieved fame at the age of twelve when he won first prize at the 1922 Grenada *cante jondo* competition organised by Manuel de Falla and Federico García Lorca. That same year performed twice at Seville's *Reina Victoria* theatre followed by the *Centro* in Madrid. Toured Spain many times thereafter. In 1930 he, '**Niña de los Peines**' and **Pastora 'Imperio'** collaborated in a show entitled *Luces de España*, a title revived after the Civil War, when he took to producing flamenco shows himself. With §**Lola Flores**, co-produced and co-starred in *Zambra* 1944*, the pinnacle of both their careers until they split in 1950. Despite his musical capriciousness and the fact that he departed from tradition to introduce orchestral accompaniment into the realm of Andalusian song (in *La niña del fuego, La Salvaora,* etc.) '**Manolo Caracol**' is considered one of the greatest *cantaores* of all time thanks to the emotive power of his raucous, shredded, *afillá* voice and his magical *duende**. His *martinetes, siguiriyas, soleares* and many of his celebrated *fandangos* consisted of sobbing, panting gasps with a powerful emotional effect on the listener.

Carbonell, Antonio –S– (Antonio Carbonell Muñoz), b. Madrid 1969. Son of **'Montoyita'** and a brother of **'La Globo', 'La Pelota'** and **'Montoyita Hijo'**. Made his *tablao* début very young, often performing in his brother-in-law **Enrique Morente**'s shows, as well as in **'Manolo Sanlúcar'**'s *Tauromagia*. Won Madrid first prize for singing in 1986.

Carmona, Juan ('El Camborio') –G– (Juan Carmona), b. Grenada 1960. Son of guitarist **Juan 'Habichuela'**. Had long been performing as a flamenco guitarist before forming a group, *Ketama*, with **José Soto 'Sorderita'**. Participated in Madrid's *Cumbre Flamenca*, 1984–1986.

Carmona, Juan –G– (Jean-Luc Carmona), b. Lyon 1963. Gave his first recital in Marseille, 1978. Won the Jerez de la Frontera international competition in 1988 and, in 1990, the *Villa Medici Hors les Murs* prize. Having experimented widely with his instrument's potential, including within the classical and jazz genres, he has created a personal style combining modern harmonies with the authenticity of the *queja,* the visceral Gitano cry. A recent album, *Antes*, traces his artistic development between 1984 and 1998.

Carrasco, Manuela –D– (Manuela Carrasco Salazar), b. Seville 1958. Made her début at the age of ten in the *El Jaleo tablao* at Torremolinos, followed by performances in Seville's *La Cochera*. Undertook numerous tours of Europe and America and appeared in many festivals. Won the national *Cátedra de Flamencología* prize at Jerez in 1974 and the San Remo international dance prize, 1981. Took part in the first Paris flamenco festival, 1976, the Second *Cumbre Flamenca*, Madrid 1985, and the 1986 New York show, *Flamenco puro*. In the 1970s her contributions to the festival at La Puebla de Cazalla and the *Gazpacho* at Morón caused a sensation. Her presence as she faced her audience, her wolf-like eyes piercing the night, before exploding into Dionysian frenzy, was in itself an utterly unforgettable spectacle.

'El del Cepillo', Alonso –S– (Alonso Suárez de la O), Puerto de Santa María (Cadiz) 1900–1990. Brother of **Dolores, Luis** and **Juana 'del Cepillo'**. Like his brother **Luis**, an excellent non-professional singer of *siguiriyas*, and, like his two sisters (included along with him in the *Magna Antología del cante flamenco)*, of ancient *romances**.

'El Chaqueta', Antonio –S– (Antonio Fernández de los Santos), b. La Línea de la Concepción (Cadiz) 1918, d. Madrid 1980. Son of **'El Mono'** and **'La Fideíto'**, brother of the dancer **Tomás 'El Chaqueta'** and of **Adela 'La Chaqueta'**, **'El Chaleco'**, **Salvador 'Pantalón'** and **'Imperio de Granada'**. Performed in some *tablaos* but mostly privately, nonetheless he passed on his knowledge of flamenco to numerous professionals.

'El Chaquetón' –S– (José Antonio Díaz Fernández), b. Algericas 1946. Son of **'El Flecha de Cadiz'** and nephew of **Antonio 'El Chaqueta'**. Went professional at the age of fifteen. In 1964 performed at the *Zambra tablao* alongside the top artists of the day before undertaking world tours with the dance troupes of **Carmen Mora** and **María Rosa**. Won the *Enrique el Mellizo* Prize at the Cordoba competition in 1980. Recorded *Aver y hoy* in 1992. His voice and sense of rhythm make him an outstanding interpreter of the styles of Cadiz.

'El Chato', Amaya –S– (Juan Amaya Santiago), Barcelona 1937–1992. *Tablao* dance-accompanist singer equally distinguished as a continuer of **'Caracol'**'s style and as a remarkable interpreter of *soleares*.

'El Chiquetete' –S– (Antonio Cortés Pantoja), b. Algeciras (Cadiz) 1948. Grandson of the *cantaor* **'Pipoño'**, nephew of **Juan Pantoja Cortés 'El Chiquetete'** and a cousin of **Isabel Pantoja**. Began his career in a couple of trios before going on to sing in the Seville *tablao Los Gallos* and with the group *Los Bolecos* (with **'Farruco'**, **'El Negro'** and **Matilde Coral**). After winning first prize in the Mairena del Alcor Competition, 1975, he continued to sing, but, with the exception of an ad hoc performance at the 1986 Seville Biennial, no longer in the flamenco genre.

'El Chocolate' –S– (Antonio Nuñez Montoya), b. Jerez de la Frontera (Cadiz) 1931. Related through his mother to the great **Montoya** family (see **'El Farruco'**, etc.). From the age of nine sang in the inns of Seville's la Alameda de los Hércules district where he lived from earliest childhood; by the late 1950s was making a name for himself at *cante* festivals. The peculiar timbre of his voice, at once nasal and vibrant, is perfectly suited to the 'most Gitano' song styles: *martinetes, siguiriyas, soleares, bulerías* and *tangos*; it is one of those 'odd' voices, forged by Gitano suffering, a rebel voice that 'hurts'.

'El Chozas' –S– (Juan José Vargas Vargas), Lebrija (Seville) 1903–1974. An agricultural labourer, he sang only at private gatherings, yet left a legacy of *romances* in the traditional style and of truly original *bulerías* and *soleares*, thankfully taken up and carried on by a number of young professionals.

'La Chunga' –D– (Micaela Flores Amaya), b. Marseille 1938. Danced in the bars of Barcelona from the age of six before going on, in the 1950s, to perform in *tablaos* and on the Mediterranean coast. In 1958, on her return from her first American tour, gave a concert in Barcelona's *Liceo* theatre, followed by numerous world tours. Opened Barcelona's *El Cordobés tablao* before taking on the starring role at Madrid's *Café de Chinitas* in 1977. Her barefoot dancing, a very personal combination of art and spontaneity, has brought her worldwide fame.

'El Cojo', Pavón –S– (Juan Pavón Suárez) Puerto Real (Cadiz), 1895–1987. Son of a Gitano blacksmith from Triana and of the dancer **'La Curra',** he worked as a barber in Puerto Real and only ever sang at private gatherings. Nonetheless exerted great influence on professionals of the stature of **'Mairena'** and **'Caracol'**.

'El Colorao, Frasco' –S– (Francisco Ortega), b. Gelves (Seville) late eighteenth century, d. Seville mid nineteenth century. Related through his wife to the '**Cagancho'** family, today recognised as the re-creator of the most ancient of the Triana *siguiriya* styles, currently known as *el Remedio*.

Cortés, Carmen –D– (Carmen Cortés), b. Barcelona 1957. Prima ballerina of **Mario Maya**'s *Teatro Gitano-Andaluz*, starred in *¡Ay! Jondo* in 1980. Three years later took part in the *Aranza* theatre troupe's *Dialogos del Amargo*; the following year, 1984, launched her own group at the Madrid *Cumbre Flamenca*.

Cortés, Joaquín –D– (Joaquín Cortés), b. Cordoba 1969. Initiated into the dance at a tender age by his uncle **Cristóbal Reyes**, joined the *Ballet Nacional de España* at fifteen, and received both classical and flamenco training there. Appointed principal dancer (*bailarín*) at twenty, quickly asserted his independence, launching a sensational solo career on the crest of that punchy hybrid, 'new wave' flamenco.

Cortés, Paco –G– (Francisco Cortés Urbano), b. Grenada 1957. Initially specialising in dance accompaniment, performed in this capacity with

Mario Maya's troupe and in the stage shows *Camelamos Naquerar* and *¡Ay! Jondo,* before switching to accompanying such great *cantaors* as **Diego Clavel**, **Enrique Morente** and **Carmen Linares**.

'El Culata, Pepe' –S– (José Bermúdez Vega), b. Seville 1911, d. Madrid 1946. A descendant of '**Curro Puya'** and brother of **Enrique 'El Culata'**. Won first prize in the 1936 national *fandango* competition organised by *Circo Price* in Madrid. Member of the *Zambra tablao* troupe, 1957–1975. A great interpreter of the *martinetes* and *siguiriyas* of Triana, as well as of the *soleares* associated with the great Alcalá singer **'La Roezna'**.

'Curro de Jerez' –G– (Francisco Fernández Loreto), b. Jerez de la Frontera 1949. Son of **'El Sernita'**, made his début aged fourteen when **Antonio**'s troupe toured England and America. Later toured the Soviet Union with the dancer **'Blanca del Rey'** and Japan with **'José Miguel'**. Has given concerts in France and Italy and performed at Madrid's *Cumbre Flamenca* in 1985 and 1986.

Donday, Santiago –S– (Santiago Donday Macías), b. Cadiz 1932. Son of **'Seis Reales'** and the singer **María 'Sabina'** (María Macías Moreno). Inheritor and guardian of the ancient styles of Jerez passed on by his paternal great-uncle **'Farrabú', Donday** was a blacksmith by trade and only sang at intimate gatherings; he did, however, record for José Manuel Caballero Bonald's *Archivo del cante flamenco*, released in 1969.

'Duquende' –S– (Juan Cortés), b. Sabadell (Barcelona) 1965. Discovered by **'Camarón'** at the tender age of nine, began a prolific recording career in 1988, accompanied by such names as **'Manzanita'** and **'Tomatito'**.

'Durse, Curro' –S– (Francisco Fernández Boigas), Cadiz, nineteenth century. Credited with the invention of three styles of *siguiriyas*.

'Encueros', Juan –S– (Juan Ortega Vargas), Puerto Real (Cadiz), nineteenth century. Brother of **'Curro Pabla'** and **'El Fillo'**. His tragic death by stabbing was the inspiration for a very famous *siguiriya* by the latter: *Mataste a mi hermano! / no t'he e perdoná / tu lo mataste liao en su capa! / sin jacerte ná.* ('You killed my brother! / I won't forgive you / you killed him, wrapped in his cloak / he had done nothing to you.')

'Faico' –D, S– (Francisco Manzano Heredia), b. Madrid 1932. Son of **'El Pelao Viejo'**, nephew of **'El Gato'**, brother of **'Juan El Pelao'** and **'El**

Fati'. Made his début at the age of twelve in **Concha Piquer**'s troupe. Joined **Pilar López**' ballet in 1947 before touring with **§Lola Flores** 1950–1971, beginning with London and Paris. Awarded the Jerez *Cátedra de Flamencología* national prize for dance, 1973.

'Farina', Rafael –S– (Rafael Antonio Salazar Motos), b. Martín Amor (Salamanca) 1923, d. Madrid 1995. Began singing in the bars of Salamanca at a very early age, introduced to Madrid audiences in the late 1940s. Toured Spain and abroad with **Conchita Piquer**. His distinctive style became very popular in the 1950s, when he enjoyed ever-growing popularity. Dubbed 'The Gypsy King', he continued to perform right through the 1980s; his shows frequently ended with him being carried out on the shoulders of his adoring fans, a practice usually reserved for bullfighters. His most creative work was in the *fandango* genre.

'El Farruco' –D– (Antonio Montoya Flores), b. Pozuelo de Alarcón (Madrid) 1936, d. Seville 1997. Grandnephew of **Ramón Montoya**, son of **'La Farruca'**. First performed in the **'Manolo Caracol'/§Lola Flores** troupe and in various *tablaos*, among them the *Guajiro* in Seville, before joining the **Pilar López** troupe in 1955 and switching, in 1965, to that of **José Greco**. Shortly afterwards, founded *Los Bolecos* with **Matilde Coral** and **José 'El Negro'**. In 1977 he and his two daughters, **'Las Farrucas'**, joined forces as **Los Farrucos**. Performed at the Seville Exposition, 1992, and received the Eighth *Compás del Cante* prize. Following the tragic death of his son **'El Farruquito'**, it is **'El Mani'**, his grandson, who carries on his dancing style, a mélange of expressivity, sublimated rage and *duende* that defies categorisation. Rarely has a dancer of such girth inspired so much emotion.

'Fernanda de Utrera' –S– (Fernanda Jiménez Peña), b. Utrera (Seville) 1923. Granddaughter of the celebrated **'Pinini'** (who achieved a solid reputation as a *cantaor* without ever performing professionally), and sister of **'Bernarda de Utrera'**, a *festera* singer, **Fernanda** made her professional début in 1955 in the festivals of the province of Seville. Exercised her talents in many Madrid *tablaos* and performed in the Spanish pavilion at the 1965 World's Fair in New York before taking part in **Manuela Vargas**' tours. Today, she is the uncontested queen of the *soleá*: the honours and distinctions bestowed upon her are beyond counting. Her voice veers from shattered sobbing to explosive rage: raucous, jagged, overflowing with the mysterious 'black sounds' of Gitano song.

Fernández, Encarnación –S– (Encarnación Fernández Fernández), b. Torrevieja (Alicante) 1948. Daughter of guitarist **Antonio Fernández**, winner of the *Lámpara Minera* at the 1979 and 1980 *Festivales de La Unión*, interprets the songs of the Levante, and most especially the *mineras**, in an unforgettable, authentically Gitano, voice.

Fernández, Esperanza –S, D– (Esperanza Fernández Vargas), b. Seville 1966. Daughter of the singer **Curro Fernández**, made her début at thirteen with the family group *Los Fernández* before going solo in **Mario Maya**'s show *Amargo*. Capable of interpreting the songs of Manuel de Falla with full orchestral accompaniment, **Esperanza** remains authentically Gitano and her star continues to rise in the firmament of the purest flamenco. Her brother **Paco Fernández**, a guitarist with a very effective, deeply personal style, is her best accompanist, while her youngest brother, dancer **José Fernández** is endeavouring to reconcile the traditional style of **'El Farruco'** with some of the most modern trends in the genre.

'El Fillo' –S– (Francisco Ortega Vargas), Puerto Real (Cadiz) 1820–1878. Known to us through the testimonies of a number of contemporaries, among them Antonio Machado y Álvarez 'Demofilo', and Serafín Estébanez Calderón who heard him in Triana in 1838. He is credited with the invention of *'de cambio'* seguiriyas*, known as *cabales**. A number of his *cantes* have survived to this day, among them a *caña**, three *cabales* and a *siguiriya* describing the murder of his brother **'Juan Encueros'** (see above). The huskiest, most raucous flamenco singing voice, *'afillá'*, is named after him.

'El Flecha de Cadiz' –S– (Antonio Díaz Soto), b. Cadiz 1869, d. Madrid 1982. Having started off in bullfighting, by 1927 he had switched to singing flamenco in the *ventas** and *tablaos* he frequented. Winner of the Fourth Cordoba Flamenco Art Competition for Cadiz styles, in 1965. Passed on the art of interpreting the songs of his province to his son Manuel, known as **'El Flecha Hijo'**.

§**Flores, Lola** –S– (Dolores Flores Ruiz), b. Jerez de la Frontera 1923, d. Madrid 1995. §**Lola Flores** was not Gitano by birth; she claimed her maternal grandfather was Gitano but the subject remains shrouded in uncertainty. What mattered for her was to be *Gitana de adentro,* Gypsy in the heart and gut, which she indubitably was in both style and temperament. She began performing at a very young age at festivals in her native town before making her professional début at the *Villamarta* theatre in 1939. Toured Spain many times before teaming up with **'Manolo Caracol'** for *Zambra*, a show that enjoyed triumphant success from 1945–1952, when they broke up. The following year she set up a troupe of her own with **'El Pescaílla'**, the singer/guitarist she subsequently married. More a popular singer than a strictly flamenco one, she owed her international success to her volcanic temper and unaffected personality.

'Frascola, Perico' –S– (Pedro Serrano Carrasco), Sanlúcar de Barrameda (Cadiz), 1833–1915. Married to the dancer **'La Tuerta'**. Credited with the invention of a very particular *seguiriya* style and with popularising another (attributed to **'El Porío'**, another singer from the same locality), he was also famed as a singer of *martinetes* and *cantiñas**.

'Frijones, Curro' –S– (Francisco Antonio Vargas), b. Jerez de la Frontera, nineteenth century, d. Seville, early twentieth century. A butcher by trade, he performed only at intimate gatherings, yet is nonetheless considered the composer of a particular *soleá*, many versions of which now exist, and of *Comparito mio Cuco*, a *siguiriya* sometimes attributed to **'Juanichi El Manijero'** and passed on by **'Parrilla'** to §**'La Piriñaca'**.

'El Funi', Miguel –S, D– (Miguel Peña Vargas), b. Lebrija (Seville), 1939. Has performed on the stages of Canada, the United States and Israel in the company of his cousin, guitarist **Pedro 'Bacán'**. Won the Jerez *Festival de la Bulería*, 1960. His distinctive sense of *compás* enables him to play about with tempo with astonishing ease.

'El Gallina' –S– (Rafael Romero Romero), b. Andújar (Jaén) 1910, d. Madrid 1991. Sang and danced in the cafés of his native town before moving to Madrid to perform in the inns and *tablaos* of the day. Employed at the *Zambra* from 1954, took part in recording the first ever *Antología del Cante Flamenco*. Toured with **Vicente Escudero, Teresa and Luisillo** and **José Greco** and featured for many years at the *El Catalán tablao* in Paris. Despite his fame, died in destitution having lost the voice that had once veered subtly between almost metallic grating and the smoothness of silk.

'El del Gastor', Diego –G– (Diego Flores Amaya), b. Arriate (Malaga) 1908, d. Morón de la Frontera (Seville) 1973. Rarely played beyond the confines of intimate private or family gatherings, yet achieved international fame and inspired imitators in Japan and the United States. His idiosyncratic style was in direct contrast to fashionable virtuosity and speed; his was a totally Oriental manner of making the instrument speak from its depths, often through the use of repetitive, always exhilarating, riffs.

'Gastor, Paco del' –G– (Francisco Gómez Amaya), b. Morón de la Frontera (Seville) 1944. Nephew and best disciple of **Diego 'El del Gastor'**, from whom he inherited his very Gitano style in which the guitar confines itself to expressing pure emotion in the service of song. Preferred accompanist of **Fernanda** and **Bernarda 'de Utrera'**. Winner of the 1984 *Giraldillo del Toque* prize at the Third Seville Biennial and participant in the Third *Cumbre Flamenca*, Madrid 1986.

'La Gazpacha' –S– (María Amaya Fajardo), Grenada 1903–1961. Daughter of the guitarist **Fernando Amaya**, sister of **Josefa**, **Paca** and **Miguel Amaya**. Won a prize for her interpretation of *bulerías* and *tarantas** at the 1922 Grenada Competition organised by Manuel de Falla and Federico García Lorca; she was also an outstanding singer of *saetas**. Performed in the *tablaos* of Andalusia, toured America with **Vicente Escudero** and sang with **Manolo Amaya**'s *Zambra* up to three days before she died. Was the last interpreter of the type of song known as *la zarabandilla*.

'La Gilica (or **Jilica**) **de Marchena'** –S– (María del Carmen Reyes Torres), b. Marchena (Seville) 1866, d. Ècija 195?. Wife of **Juan Jiménez Jiménez 'El Chindo'**, sister of *cantaor* **'Juanerillo de Marchena'** and mother of **Juan Jiménez Reyes 'El Cuacua'**. Never sang professionally but is credited with the composition of two danceable *soleares*.

'El Gloria' –S– (Rafael Ramos Antúnez), b. Jerez de la Frontera (Cadiz) 1893, d. Seville 1954. Nephew of the *cantaor* **'Cabeza' (Francisco Fernández Ramos)**, brother of **'La Pompi'** and **'La Sorda'**. Following his début at private gatherings in Jerez, went on to perform in the *cafés cantantes* of Seville, eventually touring Spain with some of the greatest names of his day. Performed in **'La Argentinita'**'s show *Las calles de Cadiz*, 1933-1934. A master of the *bulerías* of Jerez and a major composer of *saetas*, he is credited with the invention of the *villancico flamenco**.

'El Gordo Viejo' –S– (Enrique Ortega Díaz), Cadiz, nineteenth century. Father of **Enrique 'El Gordo'**, **'El Águila'**, **'Paquiro'**, **Gabriela**, **Chano**, **Manuel** and **Rita Ortega**, founder of the great Ortega dynasty with as many great bullfighters as celebrated flamenco artists, from

Rafael 'El Gallo' to **'Manolo Caracol'**, not to mention its links through marriage with other great flamenco families such as that of **Enrique 'El Mellizo'** (Jiménez) and **'Niña de los Peines'** (Pavón).

'Habichuela, Tío José' –S, G– (José Carmona Fernández), b. Lachar (Grenada) 1909, d. Grenada 1986. Son of **'Habichuela El Viejo'**. Singer and guitarist, performed in taverns with his daughter **'Tía Marina'** (María Carmona Fernández, 1911–1990). Storehouses of the styles of the Sacromonte region, particularly *tangos*, **'Tío José'** and **'Tía Marina'** only ever performed at intimate gatherings and a few local festivals.

'Habichuela', Juan –G– (Juan Carmona Carmona), b. Grenada 1923. Son of **'Tío José'** (see above) and brother to **Luis** and **Pepe** (below), made an early début as a dancer in the **Mario Maya** company in Sacromonte before switching to the guitar. It was as a guitarist that he joined **'Gracia del Sacromonte'**'s troupe before going on to perform in Madrid in the *El Duende* and *Torres Bermejas tablaos*. Accompanied **Rafael 'Farina'** and **'Manolo Caracol'** before touring America with **'Fosforito'**. Winner of the guitar section of the 1974 Cordoba National Competition, took part in the Third Seville Biennial, 1984, and in the *Flamenco puro* show in New York, 1986. Though he has been threatening to retire, he remains one of the *cantaores*' favourite accompanists due to his musicality, his sense of *compás*, and his personal qualities, particularly his serenity. Won the Eleventh *Compás del Cante*, 1995.

'Habichuela', Luis –G– (Luis Carmona Carmona), b. Grenada 1947. Son of **'Tío José'**. Began his professional career at fourteen as a singer in **'La Chunga'**'s troupe, switching to guitar when his voice broke. Played in various Madrid *tablaos* before joining numerous tours of Spain and abroad. Took part in *Cumbre Flamenca*, Madrid 1984 and 1985, and in the Third Seville Biennial, 1984.

'Habichuela, Pepe' –G– (José Antonio Carmona Carmona), b. Grenada 1944. Made his début in the *Torres Bermejas tablao* in Madrid, 1964. Subsequently toured with **Valderrama**, **Pepe 'Marchena'**, **'Camarón'**, and with **Enrique Morente** whom he accompanied on an album dedicated to the memory of **Antonio Chacón** issued by the Ministry of Culture in 1975. Also recorded with **Fernanda** and **Bernarda 'de Utrera'**, **'Jarrito'**, **'El Cabrero'**, **Rafael Heredia** and **Carmen 'Linares'** before going solo in 1983.

Heredia, Andrès –G– (Andrès Heredia Santiago), b. Madrid 1924. Son of **'El Bizco'**, nephew of **Pepe Heredia**, brother of **'Maraquilla'**, father of **Antonio Heredia López** and uncle of **Antonio Amaya Heredia**. Made his début at thirteen in the troupe of dancer **Tomás 'El Chaqueta'**. Accompanied **'La Niña de los Peines'**, **Vallejo**, **Cepero**, **'Manolo Caracol'**, among others. Part of the team at the *Zambra tablao* 1956–1975 before joining that of the *Café de Chinitas*. Note that the **Heredias** are one of the great flamenco families, with many branches: **Heredia Bermúdez**, **Heredia Cortés**, **Heredia Fernández**, **Heredia Flores**, **Heredia Maya**, **Heredia Santiago**, **Amaya Heredia**, **Fernández Heredia**, **Ortega Heredia**, **Montoya Heredia** and so on.

Heredia, Yolanda –D– (Yolanda Heredia), b. Seville 1967. Daughter of singer **Jesús Heredia**. Began dancing at the age of nine. Appeared in many of Seville's *tablaos* and as part of *La Familia Heredia* before joining **Mario Maya**'s troupe. Winning the *La Malena* prize in Cordoba in 1989 confirmed her as one of the great dancers of our time.

'Imperio' Pastora –D– (Pastora Rojas Monje), b. Seville 1889, d. Madrid 1979. Daughter of **'La Mejorana'**, a somewhat ephemeral dancer of the *cafés de cante* who refused to teach her the art. Made her début at thirteen in Madrid's *Salón Japonés*, whence her stage name. Pursued her career in the cafés and theatres of Madrid, Seville, Cordoba and Barcelona before touring abroad. Went into retirement 1928-1934, then, with her son-in-law the bullfighter Gitanillo de Triana as her manager, relaunched herself at Madrid's *Palacio de la Música*, the *Coliseum*, and *La Capitana* cabaret. Danced with the **Pilar López** company in 1946. Went back into retirement in 1959. She was particularly renowned for her hand movements, and appears to have initiated the fashion for performing certain flamenco dances in the *bata de cola* (full-length flounced dress).

'El Indio Gitano' (**'El Moro'**) –S– (Bernardo Silva Carrasco), b. Miajada (Cáceres) 1940. A member of **'La Chunga'**'s, **Antonio**'s, **'El Farruco'**'s, and **'El Güito'**'s troupes, took part in **'Manolo Sanlúcar'**'s *Tauromagia* (1988) and recorded *Nací gitano por la gracia de Dios* in 1994. Possesses an *afillá* voice similar to that of **'Tío Borrico'**, used to best advantage in the styles of Estremadura as well as in *tonás*, *siguiriyas* and *soleares*.

'Jarrito' –S– (Roque Montoya Heredia), San Roque (Cadiz) 1925–1995. Brother of two other **'Jarritos'**, **Antonio**, also a singer, b. 1912, and

Joaquín, a dancer, b. 1916, and uncle of **Pedrito Montoya**. Following his début as a dancer, moved to Madrid to sing at the *Villa Rosa*. Was a member of **Pacita Tomás'** and **Pilar López'** troupes and recorded for the first *Antología del Cante Flamenco* (1954). Performed in the *Zambra* and *El Corral de la Morería tablaos* before forming a group of his own. Went on tour with **'La Chunga'** in 1959 and sang for the great **Carmen Amaya** in New York. Spent the 1960s performing in various Madrid *tablaos* and touring abroad, then opened a *tablao* of his own in Marbella. Moved to Mexico in the early 1980s, returning to Spain in 1985 to perform again at the *Torres Bermejas*. **'Jarrito'** is a consummate and scrupulously orthodox singer.

'Niño Jero, Periquín' –G– (Pedro Carrasco Romero), b. Jerez de la Frontera (Cadiz) 1954. Son of singer/guitarist **'El Jero'** (Manuel Carrasco Jiménez). Made his début in the *ventas* of the Jerez region, accompanying **'El Borrico'**, ***'La Piriñaca'** and other local singers before going on to perform in festivals and in the stage productions *Macama Jonda* and *La tierra lleva el compás*, eventually joining and touring abroad with *Los Montoyas*, with whom he performed at the 1986 *Cumbre Flamenca* in Madrid.

'Jerónimo' –G– (Jerónimo Maya Maya), b. Madrid 1977. Son of guitarist **Felipe Maya**. Dubbed 'the Mozart of flamenco', studied at Madrid's *Conservatorio Superior de Música* before giving his first concert at the age of nine and was still very young when he took part in the Seville Biennial and the tribute to **'Sabicas'** at New York's Carnegie Hall. Has given a great many concerts abroad; took part in the Seventh *Caja Madrid* festival, 1999. His younger brother **Leo Maya**, b. 1980, appears to have an equally bright professional future.

Jiménez is the name of a great Gitano family (or rather, group of families) which has been producing flamenco artists since the nineteenth century, among them singers such as **'El Mellizo'**, **'El Morcilla'**, **Fernanda** and **Bernarda 'de Utrera'**, dancers like **Josefa** and **Regla Jiménez**, and guitarists like **'Melchor de Marchena'**. The tradition carries on today with a host of young artists, including the outstanding **Antón**, **Miguel** and **Ramón Jiménez** (who belong to three different families).

'Josele' –D– (José Heredia Escudero), b. Orihuela (Alicante), 1930. Father of **'La Bali'**, **Luisa** and **Marta Heredia**, **'Josele Hijo'** and **'El Boli'**, father-in-law of **Enrique Pantoya**, **Enrique 'de Melchor'** and

Vicente Soto. Made his début with **Concha Piquer**'s troupe before touring with §**Lola Flores**, **Valderrama**, **Gloria Romero**, etc. Performed in Madrid's principal *tablaos* before touring America in the 1960s with **José Greco**'s troupe.

'Niño Josele' –G– (Juan José Heredia Heredia), b. Almería 1974. Son of singer and guitarist **'Josele'** (José María Heredia Torres). Won the young flamenco artists' prize in 1989 and participated in the Seville Biennial the following year. Joined **'Tomatito'**'s group in 1992. Since 1993 has been giving concerts with his own group, in Norway, Switzerland, Italy and Germany. His first album, *Calle Ancha*, was produced in France in 1994. A sensitive and inspired young guitarist, **'Niño Josele'**'s future looks very bright indeed.

'Joselero' –S– (Luis Torres Cadiz), b. La Puebla de Cazalla (Seville) 1910, d. Morón de la Frontera (Seville) 1985. Brother of **'Joselero'** (**'Niño de la Puebla'**), father of **'El Andorrano'**, **'Fernandillo de Morón'** and **'Diego de Morón'**. Performed exclusively at intimate gatherings until the 1950s, when he began to give occasional concerts and to appear in a Barcelona *tablao* and at Andalusian festivals. The 1975 *Gazpacho de Morón* included a tribute to him.

'Joselito de Lebrija' –S– (José Antonio Valencia Vargas), b. Barcelona 1975. Although born in Catalonia, the singer's background and personal experience led him to identify completely with the styles of Lebrija. Demonstrated astonishing maturity and vocal qualities from a very early age. Appeared in *Chachipén*, a stage show directed by **Manuel 'de Paula'**, in 1994.

'Juane, Tío' –S– (Juan Fernández Navarro), Jerez de la Frontera (Cadiz) 1920-1995. A blacksmith by trade, sang only at intimate gatherings until the 1980s when his son **'El Niño de Jerez'** had the idea of putting on a stage show entitled *La fragua de Tío Juane* ('Tío Juane's Forge'), recreating the atmosphere of the family smithy in which he, his father and his brother **'El Gordo'** (**Manuel Fernández**) all sang. **'Tío Juane'** also featured in *Los últimos de la fiesta*, a show which raised funds for flamenco artists in their old age.

'Juanichi El Manijero' –S– (Juan Fernández Carrasco), Jerez de la Frontera (Cadiz) nineteenth-twentieth century. Father of **'El Tati'**, **'Tío Parrilla'** and **Gregorio 'Parrilla'**, uncle of **'El Borrico'**, grandfather of **'Parrilla de Jerez'**, **Juan 'Parrilla'** and **Ana 'Parrilla'**. Performed exclusively at intimate gatherings, yet mixed with the greatest artists of his time. His name is indelibly associated with *Comparito mio Cuco*, a *siguiriya* reputed to be extremely difficult to perform.

'Juaniquí' –S– (Juan Moreno Jiménez), b. Jerez de la Frontera (Cadiz) 1862, d. Sanlúcar de Barrameda (Cadiz) 1946. Lived in a hut near Lebrija and only sang at intimate gatherings. Is nonetheless famed as the inventor of at least five styles of *soleares*.

'Juliana, Tío Luis el de La' –S– (Luis Montoya Garcés), Jerez de la Frontera (Cadiz), eighteenth century. The earliest flamenco *cantaor* whose name has come down to us. Said to have been a water-bearer in Jerez and mentor to **'El Fillo'** to whom he taught his *polos*, cañas, siguiriyas, livianas** and *tonás*.

'La Kaita' –S– (María de los Ángeles Salazar), b. Badajoz 1963. Began her singing career at private parties at the age of nine. Performed in Madrid's *Ateneo* and at the Seville Biennial in the late 1980s and, in 1990, at the Eighteenth Congress of Flamenco at Badajoz. Took part in Tony Gatlif's film *Latchó Drom*, 1993. *Jaleos** and *tangos*, the Gitano songs of Estremadura, are her specialty, but her voice and tormented temperament predispose her to a flamenco repertoire in the **'Camarón'** style.

'Lacherna', Joaquín –S– (Joaquín Loreto La Serna) Jerez de la Frontera (Cadiz), nineteenth-twentieth century. Uncle of **Manuel 'Torre'**. Credited with composing a number of *siguiriyas* passed on by **Manuel 'Torre'** and **'Agujetas El Viejo'**.

'El Lebrijano' –S– (Juan Peña Fernández), b. Lebrija (Seville) 1941. Son of **'La Perrata'**, nephew of **'El Perrate'** and brother of guitarist **Pedro Peña**. Began his musical career aged sixteen as a guitarist in **Paco Cepero**'s company, then went on to sing in the *tablaos* of Seville and Madrid. Following several tours abroad with the **Antonio Gades** troupe, took to performing in theatres and at various festivals. Starred in *Persecución*, Francisco Suárez' show built around the writings of poet Félix Grande, 1979, and in *Encuentro*, accompanied by an Arabo-Andalusian band from Tangier and guitarist **Paco Cepero**, 1985. Recorded *Casablanca*, a collection of Arab-flamenco songs, in 1998. His personality, exceptional vocal qualities and audacious innovations have made him one of the most admired, as well as one of the most controversial, singers of our time.

'Lole' –S– (Dolores Montoya Rodríguez), b. Seville 1954. Daughter of **Juan Montoya** and **'La Negra'**. Began her career in the *tablaos* of Madrid and Seville. From 1972 performed with her husband, guitarist **Manuel Molina Jiménez**, creating an *aflamencado** version of popular song that instantly enjoyed enormous success. After several triumphant years, the couple split up and **'Lole'** more or less disappeared from the flamenco scene. She did, however, give a concert, in Arabic and accompanied by the *El Hilal* band, in homage to Oum Kalsoum, in 1989. **'Lole'** and **Manuel** occasionally get back together for concerts; in 1994 they made a new album in the same style as their earlier work.

'La Luz, Paco' –S– (Francisco Valencia Soto), Jerez de la Frontera, nineteenth-twentieth century. Father of **'La Sorda'** and **'La Serrana'**, brother of **'Perico Cantarote'**. Credited with composing two *siguiriyas* still sung today by certain of his descendants, such as **'El Sordera'** and **'José Mercé'**.

'Macandé' –S– (Gabriel Díaz Fernández), Cadiz 1897-1947. An itinerant sweet-seller with a flair for the outrageous, he invented a very distinctive street cry (*pregón*) to advertise his wares, as well as a *fandango* style subsequently imitated and recorded.

'La Macanita' –S– (Tomasa Guerrero Carrasco), b. Jerez de la Frontera (Cadiz) 1968. Took part in the 'Flamenco Thursdays' children's sessions held by guitarist **'Manuel Morao'** and can be seen singing, aged four, in a video from the series *Rito y Geografía del Cante*. Gave her first concert in 1983 at the Hotel *Jerez* and performed for a brief period at Madrid's *Los Canasteros tablao* before going on tour abroad. Recorded *Con el alma*, accompanied by **Moraíto Chico**, in 1995. Her superb voice, *mú flamenca*, is particularly suited to *festeros* songs.

'La Macarrona' –D– (Juana Vargas), b. Jerez de la Frontera (Cadiz) 1860, d. Seville 1947. Danced in the *cafés de cante* of Jerez, Malaga, Barcelona, Madrid and above all Seville from a very early age. Toured Spain and twice performed in Paris: in 1889 (at the Exposition's *Grand Théâtre*) and again in 1912. Her exceptional appeal earned her nicknames like *The Gypsy Empress, The Queen of Sheba* and *The Queen of the Dance*.

'Mairena', Antonio –S– (Antonio Cruz García), b. Mairea del Alcor (Seville) 1909, d. Seville 1983. Son of a Gitano blacksmith, brother of **Curro** and **Manuel 'Mairena'**. In 1924 won the flamenco *cante* competition held in Alcalá de Guadaira and six years later began his professional career at Seville's *Kursaal Internacional*, accompanied by **Javier Molina**. In the early 1940s joined **Juanita Reina's** company, switching to **Pilar López'** ballet troupe followed by stints at two Madrid taverns, *La Capitana* and *Villa Rosa*. Toured Europe with **Teresa and Luisillo's** ballet troupe in the 1950s before going on to tour most of the world with **Antonio's**. In 1962 he won the Golden Key, first prize for *cante**, at the Cordoba Competition of Flamenco Art. From this point onwards he dedicated all his energy to rehabilitating flamenco, which appeared to be in danger of dying out, and to recreating ancient styles. Co-edited, with Ricardo Molina, *Mundo y Formas del Cante Flamenco*, published Madrid 1963, followed in 1976 by his autobiography *Las confesiones de Antonio Mairena*. Notwithstanding the ill-will and controversy he inspired, particularly through his partisan championing of Gitano flamenco and because of the debate about the authenticity or otherwise of his re-creations, today he is universally recognised as the most influential *cantaor* of his time. He remains the ultimate authority with regard to orthodoxy and encyclopaedic grasp of the genre, yet he unintentionally fuelled the violent anti-Gitano backlash of the 'post-Mairena era'.

'Mairena', Manuel –S– (Manuel Cruz García), b. Mairena del Alcor (Seville) 1934. Won a *saetas* competition run by Radio Seville at the age of thirteen. In 1951, sang at the academy of **Enrique 'El Cojo'**, then toured Spain and abroad with various groups. In 1965 toured Europe and America with **Manuela Vargas'** company. Took part in **Manuel 'Morao''s** tribute to his bother **Antonio** at Vanderbilt Hall, New York, 1995. Won numerous prestigious awards over the course of his long career. A consummate performer excelling at the interpretation of those songs known as *primitive* or *Gitano*, and an unrivalled singer of *saetas*.

'La Malena' (1) –D– (Magdalena Seda Loreto), b. Jerez de la Frontera (Cadiz) 187?, d. Seville 1956. Niece of **'La Chorrúa'**. Began her career in the *cafés cantantes* of the day, then went on tour, first with **'La Argentinita'**, then with **Concha Piquer**, before setting up her own troupe, *Malena and her Gitanos*. A legendary figure celebrated by Federico García Lorca, **'La Malena'** ended her days selling cigarettes and sunflower seeds from a street stall opposite the *Las Maravillas* bar on the Alameda de los Hércules in Seville.

'La Malena' (2) –S– (Magdalena Carrasco Amaya), b. Lebrija (Seville) 1925. Aunt of **'Curro Malena'** and mother of **Manuel** and **Antonio 'Malena'**, sang exclusively at weddings and other family gatherings.

Antonio 'de La Malena' –S– (Antonio Moreno Carrasco), b. Jerez de la Frontera (Cadiz) 1961. Son of **'La Malena'**, brother of **Manuel 'Malena'**, nephew of **Manuel** and **Juan 'Morao'** and cousin of **'Curro Malena'**. A remarkable dance accompanist and great connoisseur of the styles of Jerez. Made his first recording, *Yo soy asi, asi soy yo*, in 1997.

'Curro Malena' –S– (Francisco Carrasco Carrasco), b. Lebrija (Seville) 1945. Grandson of **'La Rumbilla'**, nephew of **'La Malena'**, cousin of **Manuel 'de Paula'**, **Manuel** and **Antonio 'Malena'**. Performed with other young *flamencos* in the villages of his native region until being taken on by Seville's *La Cuadra tablao*. In 1988, accompanied by **Pedro Bacán**, recorded *Manantial Gitano*. Winner of a great many prizes, has toured extensively and given concerts in France and Switzerland. Possesses an instinctive grasp of *compás* and, thanks to his family background, an encyclopaedic familiarity with the range of traditional styles. Excels at *soleares* and *bulerías*.

'Manolete' –D– (Manuel Santiago Maya), b. Grenada 1945. Brother of **'Marote'** and **Pepe Maya**. Began dancing in the caves of Sacromonte at the age of seven. Performed in various *tablaos* in Madrid and Andalusia before touring abroad with **María Rosa**'s ballet troupe as well as with the *Ballet Nacional de España*. Has visited Japan on numerous occasions with his own troupe.

'Manolito de María' –S– (Manuel Fernández Cruz), b. Alcalá de Gaudaira (Seville) 1904, d. Seville 1966. Nephew of **Joaquín 'de La Paula'** and **Agustín 'Talega'**, cousin of **Juan 'Talega'** and **Antonio 'Mairena'**. The fact that he only sang at intimate gatherings did not prevent him from exercising an enormous influence as a preserver of ancient styles. Specialising in the *soleares* of Alcalá, he was equally outstanding in the interpretation of *martinetes, siguiriyas, saetas* and *bulerías*, creating a form of his own for this last. His cavernously deep voice was unforgettably evocative of the cave dwellings of his forebears. Recorded for Caballero Bonald's *El Archivo del Cante Flamenco*, and some of his performances at private gatherings are included on the *Testimonios Flamencos* of the *Historia del Flamenco* (1996).

'Manzanita' –G– (José Ortega Heredia), b. Madrid 1956. Son of **'Trini Heredia'** and **Rafael Ortega**. Began his career at a very early age at *Los Canasteros tablao*, Madrid. Joined **Enrique Morente**'s group before going on to found, with **Miguelín Losada** and **'Veneno'**, the 'pop flamenco' group *Los Chorbos*. A *cantante* (music hall singer) rather than a *cantaor* (singer of flamenco), he invented the sound known as *caño roto*.

'Marchena, Melchor de' –G– (Melchor Jiménez Torres), b. Marchena (Seville) 1907, d. Madrid 1980. Started off in the 1930s playing at private gatherings, where he accompanied the major figures of the day. Subsequently toured Spain and America, initially with **Concha Piquer**, then with **'Manolo Caracol'**, before being taken on as principal guitarist at Madrid's *Los Canasteros tablao*. Winner of the 1966 *Cátedra de Flamencología* National Flamenco Guitar Award, he was the preferred accompanist of both **'Manolo Caracol'** and **Antonio 'Mairena'**, appreciated equally for his masterful accompaniment, his sonority and the profoundly *flamenco* spirit of his style.

'María Soleá' –S, D– (María de la Soledad Fernández Monje), b. Jerez de la Frontera (Cadiz) 1932. Sister of **'Terremoto'**, niece of **'Tía Juana La del Pipa'**, **'Tío Parrilla'** and **'El Borrico'**. Following a very early début in various theatres and *tablaos*, abandoned her professional career and did not reappear in public until after her brother **'Terremoto'**'s death in 1981. Recorded *Embrujo del Cante*, 1991. Although her voice is somewhat reminiscent of her brother's, her style is entirely her own.

'Mariquilla' –D– (María Guardia Gómez), b. Grenada 1949. Daughter of guitarist **'Pataperro'** and of singer/dancer **'Carajarapa'**. Performed from the age of six in the caves of Sacromonte, where she was born, going on to various theatres and *tablaos* in Spain and France, before undertaking tours abroad with her own troupe. Managed a flamenco school in Madrid before teaching dance at the University of Grenada.

'Marote' –G– (Juan Santiago Maya), b. Grenada 1936. Brother of **'Manolete'** and of **Pepe Maya**. Started off as a dancer in the *zambras* of Sacromonte before turning to the guitar and joining **Rafael 'Farina'**'s troupe at the age of eighteen. Based at the *Torres Bermejas tablao* in Madrid 1960-65, during which period he made several trips abroad with **Carmen Amaya**'s troupe, particularly to the United States where, with the **Antonio 'Gades'** ballet, he performed at the 1964 World's Fair. Also toured with **Manolo Várgas** and **María Rosa** and worked on numerous occasions with the *Ballet Nacional de España*. His very personal style makes him one of the most original guitarists of our era.

'El Marruro', Diego –S– (Diego Monje), Jerez de la Frontera (Cadiz) 1850-1920. Created a very characteristic and moving style of *siguiriya* interspersed with numerous *¡Ay!*s.

Maya, Mario –D– (Mario Maya Fajardo), b. Cordoba 1937. Father of the dancer **Belén Maya**. Danced in the caves of Grenada's Sacromonte from earliest childhood. Following a brief stint at **'El Estampío'**'s academy in Madrid became associated with the *Villa Rosa colmao** where he performed in several shows with **'Manolo Caracol'** before moving on to various *tablaos* – the *Zambra*, *Corral de la Morería* and *Torres Bermejas* – and touring abroad with **Pilar López**, **'La Chunga'** and **María Baena**. From 1965 to 1966 he was based in New York, where he gave numerous concerts, then returned to Spain and formed the *Trío Madrid* with **Carmen Mora** and **'El Güito'**. From 1974, he was the creative force behind numerous shows combining ballet and theatre to bring the written word to the stage, among them *Ceremonial*, based on a text by Juan de Loxa; 1976's *Camelamos Naquerar* (the title, in the Gitano language Caló, means 'We Want to Speak Out') by José Heredia Maya; *¡Ay! Jondo* (1980, also based on a Juan de Loxa text); *Amargo* (1982, around the poetry of García Lorca); and finally, in 1992, *Tres movimientos flamencos*, for which he won that year's national dance award. Founded a Centre for Flamenco Activities in Seville, 1983, devoted to teaching dance. Appointed artistic director of the *Ballet Andaluz*, 1995.

Maya, Tere –D– (Teresa Maya Cortés), b. Grenada 1920. Granddaughter of **María 'La Chata de la Jampona'**, daughter of **'El Cotorrero'** and **Juana 'la del Caganchín'**, sister of **Juanele Maya**, **Bienvenido Maya** and **'La Lili'**, mother of **Paquita Maya** and aunt of **Toni Maya**. Began dancing in earliest childhood in the caves of Sacromonte; joined **Vicente Escudero**'s troupe, with which she travelled to America, at the age of twelve. Subsequently toured with **Carmen Amaya**, **'La Pilina'**, and, as prima ballerina, travelled Europe and America with **José Greco**'s dance troupe. Performed in Madrid's *Café de Chinitas* for over a decade before going into retirement in the 1980s. Her brother **'Juanele'**, also once part of **José Greco**'s ballet troupe, switched from the dance to guitar in the 1970s.

Medrano, Ramón –S– (Ramón Medrano Fernández), b. Sanlúcar de Barrameda (Cadiz) 1906, d. Seville 1984. Grandson of the dancer **'La Bizca'**. A butcher by trade, rarely performed in public. Was nonetheless a treasure-house of the most authentic songs of his region: *siguiriyas, tonás* and the famous *cantiñas* known as *Las Mirris*.

'Melchor, Enrique de' –G– (Enrique Jiménez Ramírez), b. Marchena (Seville) 1951. Son of **'Melchor de Marchena'** and married to dancer/singer **Dolores Heredia Bermúdez 'La Josela'**. Following his début at the age of fifteen in Madrid's *Los Canasteros tablao*, has made very many tours abroad, particularly to the United States where, with **José Menese**, he performed at the Theatre of the United Nations. Both an excellent accompanist and an inspired solo performer.

'El Mellizo' –S– (Enrique Jiménez Fernández), Cadiz 1848-1906. Father of **Antonio 'El Mellizo'**, **'El Morcilla'** and **'Carlota'**. Employed in the abbatoirs of Cadiz, took part in numerous bullfights, initially as *banderillero*, then as *puntillero* to Manuel Hermosilla. With rare exceptions in the *cafés cantantes* of his native city, sang only at private get-togethers. Suffering from frequent bouts of depression, he tended to wander off on his own and could be found standing on the city wall singing to the sea or outside the psychiatric asylum run by the Capuchin monks, where he sang for the patients. Created a very particular type of *malagueña** said to be inspired by Gregorian chant but which undoubtedly owes more to a very Gitano style of interpretation. He is also credited with the composition of two *siguiriyas*, three *soleares* and several *tientos**.

'Mercé', José –S– (José Soto Soto), b. Jerez de la Frontera (Cadiz) 1955. A descendant of **'Paco La Luz'**, nephew of **'El Sernita'** and **'El Sordera'**. Made his début at the age of twelve in **Manuel 'Morao'**'s 'Flamenco Thursdays' before being taken on, in 1970, by *La Cueva del Pájaro azul tablao* in Cadiz; the following year switched to Madrid's *Torres Bermejas*. Sang for the *Trío Madrid* before joining **Antonio 'Gades'**' company with which he spent the decade 1973-83 and appeared in the 1981 film, *Bodas de sangre*. Won the *La Serneta* and *Niña de los Peines* prizes at the 1986 Cordoba Competition, after which he performed in *El Café de Chinitas*, a Madrid *tablao*. Took part in *Esplendor,* staged at the Eighth Seville Biennial, in 1994, and, the following year, in Carlos Saura's film *Flamenco*. His voice, resonant with the echoes of Gitano generations, possesses the 'torn' quality of *cante jondo* at its most authentic. His natural gifts, harnessed to a perfect mastery of his art, make him one of the best *cantaores* of our age.

'El Mijita de Jerez' –S– (Alfonso Carpio Fernández), b. Jerez de la Frontera (Cadiz) 1972. Son of **'El Mijita'**, nephew of **'El Garbanzo'** and great grandson of **'El Chalao'**. Heir to the densest, purest styles of *La Plazuela*, the Gitano quarter of San Miguel, his singing is characterised by the rage and 'black notes' also associated with his cousins, the **'Agujetas'** (see above).

'El Mistela' –D– (Juan Manuel Rodríguez García), b. Los Palacios (Seville) 1965. Has performed with **'El Farruco'** and with **Mario Maya**, in whose troupe he played principal dancer in the stage productions *El amor brujo, Amargo,* and *Tiempo, amor y muerte*. Was also principal dancer, partnering **Juana Amaya**, in **Salvador Távora**'s production of *Carmen,* presented at the 1996 Seville Biennial.

'Mojama', Juanito –S– (Juan Valencia Carpio), b. Jerez de la Frontera (Cadiz) 189?, d. Madrid 1957. His career unfurled in the *colmaos* of Madrid: the *Café de Fornos, Los Gabrieles, Villa Rosa*. Thanks to the recordings he made in 1929, accompanied by **Ramón Montoya**, we can still appreciate the talent he brought to his interpretation of **'La Serneta'**'s *soleares,* **Vallejo**'s *granaína*,* and *bulerías por soleá** (see *Historia del Flamenco,* records 37, 38 and 39).

Molina, Señor Manuel ('Curro' Molina) –S– (Manuel Molina), Jerez de la Frontera (Cadiz), nineteenth century. Although his Gitano background has been questioned, his descendants, still working as butchers in Jerez, are living proof of it. He is credited with having invented three styles of *siguiriyas*.

'Tío Mollino' –S– (Manuel Arroyo Jiménez), Algeciras (Cadiz) 1913-1996. With the exception of a single album made in 1989, never sang except at private gatherings, yet this recording sufficed to bring his profound and authentic style, particularly in evidence in his treatment of *tonás, soleares*, and the *siguiriyas* of **Manuel 'Torre'**, to public attention.

Moneo, Manuel –S– (Manuel Moneo Lara), b. Jerez de la Frontera (Cadiz) 1950. Brother of **Juan 'El Torta'**, nephew of **Luis 'de Pacote'** and of **'El Chico'**, father of **'El Barullo'**. Started off in **Manuel 'Morao'**'s 'Flamenco Thursdays' before going on to perform in *peñas** and at festivals. Successor to **Manuel 'Torre'** and **Antonio 'Mairena'**, and a leading interpreter of the traditional styles of Jerez.

Montoya, Ramón –G– (Ramón Montoya Salazar), Madrid 1879-1948. Began performing professionally at the age of fourteen in the *cafés cantantes* of the capital, was principal guitarist at the *Café de la Marina* for many years before becoming official accompanist to **Antonio Chacón**, 1912-1926. During the Civil War, designer Marius de Zayas gave him the opportunity to tour France, Belgium, England and the United States. Not content with accompanying the greatest names of his era, including **'La Niña de los Peines'**, **Ramón Montoya** was one of the first guitarists to record solo, as early as the first decade of this century. His particular technique, combining virtuosity, speed and a sense of rhythm, has been much emulated.

'Morao', Manuel –G– (Manuel Moreno Jiménez), b. Jerez de la Frontera (Cadiz) 1929. Brother of **Juan 'Morao'**. From 1945 toured Spain and abroad in the companies of **'Manolo Caracol'**, **Pastora 'Imperio'**, **'La Niña de los Peines'**, §**Lola Flores** and **Carmen Amaya**. 1953-1964, lead guitarist with **Antonio**'s ballet, with which he toured the world. Began his *Jueves Flamencos* ('Flamenco Thursday') shows in 1966, and with them launched numerous budding young artists who have since achieved fame in their own right. Went back on tour with **Antonio** in 1970. In 1985, founded his own company with which he performed in the United States under the aegis of the National Theater Company. Classically and profoundly *flamenco*, the ideal accompanist, **Manuel 'Morao'** is considered one of the greatest guitarists of his time.

'Moraíto, Chico' –G– (Manuel Moreno Junquera), b. Jerez de la Frontera (Cadiz) 1956. Son of **Juan 'Morao'** and nephew of **Manuel 'Morao'**, started off in his uncle's 'Flamenco Thursdays' in 1966 before going on to perform in various Madrid *tablaos*. His album *Morao y Oro*, recorded in France in 1994, was awarded the *Prix Charles Cros*. Took part in the 1999 *Caja Madrid* festival. An excellent exponent of the Jerez style, brilliant and rhythmical, with a tendency towards a great deal of thumb work. A wonderful accompanist, also maintains a solo career.

'El Morcilla' –S– (José Enrique Jiménez Espeleta), Cadiz 1877-1929. Son of **'Enrique El Mellizo'**, brother of **Antonio** and **Carlota**. Performed in the *cafés cantantes* of Cadiz, Seville and Madrid, specialising in *siguiriyas, soleares*, Gitano *saetas* and *malagueñas*.

'**Morena, Fernando de La**' –S– (Fernando Carrasco Vargas), b. Jerez de la Frontera (Cadiz) 1945. Son of '**La Morena**' and brother of '**Curro de La Morena**'. Gifted with a very *flamenco* voice and a remarkable sense of *compás*, excels at the *bulerías* of his own *Santiago* quarter, as well as *soleares* and *fandangos*.

Moreno, 'Gabriel' –S– (José Moreno Carrillo), b. Linares (Jaén) 1941. Made his début at the age of eight in programmes on Malaga radio. After a four-year stint at New York's *Château Madrid*, returned to Madrid proper where until 1971 he performed at the *El Corral de la Morería tablao* when not touring the world with **Lucero Tena**'s group. Performed in numerous other theatrical shows before putting together his own in 1973. An electric singer ever in search of innovative forms, successor to the **Pastora** and **Tomás Pavón** schools of *soleares*, *siguiriyas*, *tonás*, *bulerías* and *tangos*. Introduced a particular type of *fandango* and some curious Gitano *tangos* from Linares.

'**Morón, Diego de**' –G– (Diego Torres Amaya), b. Morón de la Frontera (Seville) 1947. Son of '**Joselero**' and nephew of **Diego 'el del Gastor'**. Started off accompanying his father before going on tour abroad, particularly to the United States which he visits regularly; usually performs as a soloist. Took part in the Third Seville Biennial, 1984, and in the Seventh *Caja Madrid* festival in March 1999.

'**El Nano de Jerez**' –S, D– (Cayetano Fernández González), b. Jerez de la Frontera (Cadiz) 1948. Son of '**Tío Juane**'. Made his début at **Manuel 'Morao'**'s 'Flamenco Thursdays', going on from there to the *tablaos* of Seville. Won the *Niña de los Peines* prize for *bulerías* at the 1980 Cordoba Competition. In 1987 produced a show entitled *La Fragua de Tío Juane* ('Tío Juane's Forge'), co-starring with his father and his brother '**El Gordo**'. Excels at *martinetes* – the songs of the smithy – and *patrás* (singing to accompany the dance), which he alternates with concert work and festivals. Recorded *Alrreó de la fragua,* accompanied by the guitarist **Fernando Moreno**, in 1991.

'**La Negra**' –S, D– (Antonia Rodríguez Moreno), b. Oran (Algeria) 1936. Wife of dancer **Juan Montoya** and mother of '**Lole**'. In the late 1970s she and her family came together as *Los Montoyas*, performing in many festivals in Spain and abroad; one of their most impressive appearances was at the Second Seville Biennial, 1984. '**La Negra**' is an excellent interpreter of *festeros* styles, *bulerías* and *rumbas* in particular.

'El Negro del Puerto' –S– (José de los Reyes Santos), b. Puerto de Santa María (Cadiz) 1913. Though not a professional singer, has recorded on numerous occasions, including for Caballero Bonald's *Archivo del Cante Flamenco* and the *Magna Antología del cante Flamenco*. In these, he gives us a selection of his great specialty, Gitano *romances*.

'El Nitri' –S– (Tomás de Vargas Suárez), Puerto de Santa María (Cadiz) 1828-187?. Nephew of **'El Fillo'**. Undoubtedly the singer most surrounded by question marks, improbable legend and controversy. Even the date and place of his death are unclear, as are the circumstances under which he was awarded the *Llave de oro del Cante* ('Golden Key' award); it is, however, difficult to believe that this could have taken place in 1862 when he was only twelve years old. **'El Nitri'** never performed in public. Three *siguiriyas* styles are attributed to him.

Nuñez, Agustín ('El Gitano') –S– (Agustín Nuñez Fernández), b. Estepona (Malaga) 1920. Performed from a very early age in La Línea de la Concepción, graduating to the *tablaos* of Malaga, Seville, Cadiz and, in Madrid, *El Corral de la Morería* and *Las Brujas*. A marvellous interpreter of the classic styles – *siguiriyas* and *soleares* – as well as of *tientos* and *fandangos*.

Ortega, Gabriela –D– (Gabriela Ortega Feria) – b. Cadiz 1862, d. Seville 1919. Daughter of **'El Gordo Viejo'**, sister of **'El Águila'**, **Chano Ortega**, **'Paquiro'**, **Rita Ortega**, **Enrique 'El Gordo'** and **Manuel Ortega**, wife of bullfighter Fernando 'El Gallo', grandmother of the *cantaor* **'Rebujina'** and of the reciter Gabriela Ortega. Performed in the *cafés cantantes* of Cadiz and Seville.

Ortega, Rafael –D– (Rafael Ortega Monje) Seville ?-1973. Grandson of **'El Gordo Viejo'**, son of singer **Manuel Ortega Feria**, brother of **'El Almendro'** and of the dancer **Carlota Ortega Monje**. Performed in the 1929 Seville production *La copla andaluza*, followed by tours with **'Manolo Caracol'** and **'La Argentinita'**. Partnered **Pilar López** from 1934 to the outbreak of the Civil War. During the 1950s and 1960s, went back on tour, this time with **Pastora 'Imperio'**, **Pilar López**, **Concha Piquer** and §**Lola Flores**. An impetuous, profoundly Gitano dancer. (NB, not to be confused with another **Rafael Ortega**, from the same great family, who was the son of **José Ortega Morales**, husband of **Trini Heredia** and father of **'Manzanita'**.)

Ortega, Regla –D– (Regla Márquez Ortega), b. Chiclana de la Frontera (Cadiz) 1909, d. Madrid 1986. Wife of guitarist **Pepe Romera** and aunt of **'Manolo Caracol'**. Made her début aged eight, in Seville, then went on tour with various variety shows. Toured America in the 1950s, initially with a show called *Romería*, then with the **Carmen Amaya** troupe. From 1958 onwards performed in a number of Madrid *tablaos* while undertaking frequent tours abroad with **'La Singla'**'s group and others. A dancer both instinctive and classical to whom we owe many innovations, particularly in *tientos*, *polos* and *tarantos*.

'Palma, Manuel de' –G– (Manuel Fernández Castro), b. Écija (Seville) 1957. An excellent accompanist to both dance and song, has brought his own touch to the style of **Diego 'el del Gastor'**.

'Pansequito' –S– (José Cortés Jiménez), b. La Línea de la Concepción (Cadiz) 1946. Started off in the *tablaos* of Malaga where in 1963 he was noticed by **'Manolo Caracol'**, who hired him for *Los Canasteros*, his own *tablao* in Madrid. Toured Europe with **Antonio 'Gades''** troupe, then went back to the festivals and *tablaos* of Malaga, Seville and Madrid. His *afillá* voice is laden with the echoes of his mentor **'Caracol'**, yet he has evolved a *soleá* style all his own.

'La Paquera' –S– (Francisca Méndez Garrido), b. Jerez de la Frontera (Cadiz) 1934. Following her 1957 début in Madrid's *Corral de la Morería*, undertook numerous tours of Spain with shows such as *España por bulerías* (1959), *Arte español* (1960), *Carrusel de canciones* (1961), and *Ronda de canciones* (1962), among others. Also toured with **Rafael 'Farina'**. From the 1960s onwards appeared in various Madrid and Seville *tablaos* and at numerous festivals. A great specialist in *festeros* songs, in particular the Cadiz *bulería*, which she interprets in a highly personal manner.

'Paquirri el Guanté' –S, G, D– (?), b. Cadiz, d. Madrid, nineteenth century. Generally agreed to have been Gitano, little else is known of him, including his real name. Recognised as the inventor of three styles of *soleares*.

'Parrilla de Jerez' –G, D– (Manuel Fernández Molina), b. Jerez de la Frontera (Cadiz) 1945. Grandson of **'Juanichi El Manijero'**, son of **'Tío Parrilla'**, nephew of **'El Borrico'** and of **'El Sernita'**, brother of guitarist **Juan 'Parrilla'** and the dancer **Ana 'Parrilla'**. After his first public appearance at the Seville *Feria*, aged thirteen, went on to perform in various *tablaos* and to tour with a number of groups, among them **'La Paquera'**'s and that of §**Lola Flores**. Also gave concerts and recorded a solo album.

'El Parrón' –S– (Jaime Heredia Amaya), b. Grenada 1955. Grandson of blacksmith and *cantaor* **'El Parrón'** and nephew of **'Juanillo el Gitano'**. Began his career at twelve in the caves of Sacromonte and the *tablaos* of Grenada. Had a role in José Heredia Maya's show *Macama Jonda*. His characteristically Gitano voice is ideal for *siguiriyas* and *soleares*.

'Paula, Joaquín el de La' –S– (Joaquín Fernández Vargas), Alcalá de Guadaira (Seville) 1875-1933. Uncle of singers **Juan 'Talega'** and **'Manolito el de María'**. Wounded in the Cuban War, took up donkey-shearing and sang only at private gatherings. Nonetheless created three of the Alcalá *soleares*.

'Paula, Manuel de' –S– (Manuel Valencia Carrasco), b. Lebrija (Seville) 1956. Grandson of **'La Rumbilla'**, nephew of **'La Malena'**, cousin of **Manuel**, **Antonio** and **Curro 'Malena'**. First came to public attention in 1970, when he won first prize at the Mairena del Alcor competition. Has since won many more, taken part in **Mario Maya**'s shows, and given numerous concerts. An excellent interpreter of *soleares* and *bulerías*. Composed a very moving *romance* in memory of his grandmother **'La Rumbilla'**.

'Paulera de Jerez' –S– (Francisco Vargas Vargas), b. Jerez de la Frontera (Cadiz) 1922. Son of **'Paulera Viejo'** and son-in-law of §**'La Piriñaca'**. Like his father (**Francisco de Paula Vargas Dávila**, 1902–1974), only performed at intimate gatherings and when working in the fields. Gifted with a deep and very *flamenco* voice perfectly suited to the *bulerías* of the *Santiago* quarter as well as to the *siguiriyas* of **'Tío José de Paula'** passed on by his father.

Pabón (or **Pavón**) **Pastora** (**'Niña de los Peines'**) –S– (Pastora Pabón Cruz), Seville 1890-1969. Following her début at Seville's *Taberna de Ceferino*, went on to perform in Madrid and Bilbao, then returned to the *cafés cantantes* of Andalusia. Went back to Madrid in 1921, then toured with accompanist **'Habichuela'** and took part in the Grenada Festival in the Palace of Charles the Fifth. Went on a tour organised by Vendrines in 1926 and in 1928 toured Spain again, this time starring in one of her famous *óperas flamencas** with **Antonio Chacón**. After various appearances at Madrid's *Circo Price*, went on tour until 1935 and again in 1939 and 1940, then took part in **Conchita Piquer**'s show *Las calles de Cadiz*. Went into retirement but came out again in 1949 to perform, with her husband **Pepe 'Pinto'**, in *España y su cantaora*, then retired for good. In 1968, not long before she died, her statue was erected at the top of Seville's Alameda de los Hércules. **Pastora** was exceptional in the history of flamenco. A legend in her own lifetime, she remains an uncontested genius, one of flamenco's greatest voices, the most comprehensive of all singers and creator of new *cantes* such as the *garrotín** and the *bamberas**. She had the gift of transforming everything she touched into *cante jondo*; her versions of *tangos* and *peteneras** were virtually new compositions. García Lorca called her 'the sombre Hispanic genius', praising her 'moss-covered' voice of 'shadow' and 'molten tin', and her irresistible *duende*.

Pabón (or **Pavón**), **Tomás** –S– (Tomás Pabón Cruz), Seville 1893-1952. Brother of **'Niña de los Peines'** and **Arturo Pabón**, uncle of pianist Arturo Pabón. His performances were restricted to private gatherings and a few 78 RPM recordings, six of them accompanied by **'Niño Ricardo'** and three by **'Melchor de Marchena'**, thanks to which we have irrefutable proof of his genius. Lived at the worst ever time for flamenco, the era of the so-called *ópera flamenca*, a misfortune he bore with dignity and the disdain of an aristocrat who chooses poverty rather than make concessions to fashion. Noteworthy among the styles he recorded are the *siguiriyas* passed down by **Manuel 'Cagancho'**, **'La Serneta''**s *soleares*, and several type of *tonás*.

'Pelao, Juan el' –S– (?), b. Utrera (Seville), d. Seville, nineteenth century. Nephew of **'El Pelao de Utrera'** and brother of **José 'El Pelao'**. His real name, like the dates of his birth and death, are unknown. A legendary figure known through oral tradition and the anecdotes of Fernando el de Triana, he was reputedly a great master of the *martinete*.

'El Pele' –S– (Manuel Moreno Maya), b. Cordoba 1954. Having made his début in the *peñas* of Cordoba, won the 1969 Cabra competition followed by many others, but it was his awards for *soleares* and *bulerías* at the 1983 Cordoba competition that really established his reputation. Recorded an album, *Avante Claro*, with **'La Macanita'** in 1995. His voice has the 'raucous' quality *(rajo*)* proper to the basic Gitano songs – *tonás, siguiriyas, soleares, bulerías* – which he interprets with emotion, expressivity and a sure sense of *compás*.

Peña, Pedro –G, S– (Pedro Peña Fernández), b. Lebrija (Seville) 1939. Son of **'La Perrata'**, nephew of **'El Perrate'** and brother of singer **'El Lebrijano'**, a professional teacher and performer of flamenco. Accompanist to his mother, his brother, **Antonio 'Mairena'**, **Diego Clavel** and many others, has also recorded as a singer in his own right, accompanied by his cousin **Pedro 'Bacán'**. Also distinguished himself by writing and directing the flamenco stage show *Cien años de cante*.

'Peret' –G, S– (Pedro Pubill Calaf), b. Mataró (Barcelona) 1938. Having made his début in Catalonia, went on tour in Argentina and brought back a new type of *rumba* to instant acclaim. **'Peret'** is not a flamenco singer but, along with **Antonio González Batista 'El Pescaílla'**, invented the *rumba catalana* which quickly caught on in France; it has been popularised by the *Gypsy Kings* and by several French-based Gitano groups, among them *Te Kameli* and *Rumberos Catalans*.

'La Perla', Francisco –S– (Francisco Mendoza), b. Seville ca. 1850, d. ? Grandfather of **Luis 'El Compare'**. Born to a Triana blacksmith family, lived in Cadiz from earliest childhood: the two *siguiriyas* styles attributed to him are of the Cadiz school. The lyrics of one of his *siguiriyas* allude to his son's flight to Africa following a brawl: *Currito de mi alma / mándame una carta / que con saber que estás bueno / me sobra y me basta* ('Little Curro of my heart / send me a letter / just to know that you are all right / that's enough for me').

'La Perla de Cadiz' –S– (Antonia Gilabert Vargas), Cadiz 1925–1975. Daughter of singer **Rosa 'la Papera'** (Rosa Vargas Fernández) and wife of dancer/singer **'Curro de la Gamba'**. Performed in numerous *tablaos* in Madrid, Seville and Cadiz but was best known for her festival appearances and tours abroad. Considered Cadiz' greatest singer, she specialised in the city's typical song styles – *bulerías, alegrías* and other *cantiñas* – which she sang in a fluid voice full of Gitano *rajo*.

'La Perrata' –S– (María Fernández Granados), b. Utrera (Seville) 1922. Sister of **'El Perrate'**, aunt of **'Gaspar de Utrera'**, **'El Turronero'** and **Pedro 'Bacán'**, cousin of **Fernanda** and **Bernarda 'de Utrera'**, mother of **Pedro Peña** and **'El Lebrijano'**. Sang at family gatherings from earliest childhood but did not perform in public until the 1960s, when she appeared at Lebrija's *La Caracolá* festival accompanied by her son **Pedro**. An authentic and very distinctive performer of *soleares, bulerías, romances* and *alboreás**.

'**El Perate**' –S– (José Fernández Granados), Utrera (Seville) 1915–1992. Brother of '**La Perrata**'. Made his début at the Utrera *Kursaal* aged ten and went on to perform in various Seville and Madrid *tablaos* as well as at festivals. Considered one of the great masters of Utrera *soleares*.

'**El Pescaílla**' –S, G– (Antonio González Batista), b. Barcelona 1926. Father of '**Toñi La Pescaílla**', child of his first marriage to singer/dancer **Dolores Amaya Moreno**, and of Antonio, Lolita and Rosario Flores, children of his second marriage to §**Lola Flores**. Worked in Lola's group as well as in the *tablaos* of Madrid. One of the great interpreters of the *rumba*, which he stamped with his own personality.

'**Picoco**' –S, D– (Vicente Pantoja Monje), b. Jerez de la Frontera (Cadiz) 1920. Son of singer, dancer and humorist **Vicente Pantoja Antúnez**. His christening party, which lasted for three days and brought together numerous flamenco artists, was the stuff of legend around Jerez. Toured Spain and America with various groups, including that of §**Lola Flores.**

'**El Pili**' –S, D– (Alonso Méndez Heredia), b. Jerez de la Frontera (Cadiz) 1916. Uncle of '**La Paquera**', brother of *cantaor* **Eduardo Méndez Heredia** and father of **Antonio Méndez Sánchez**. Started off at intimate gatherings before taking part in shows organised by **Manuel Vallejo**, '**Manolo Caracol**' and §**Lola Flores**, '**La Paquera**', and **Sebastián Nuñez**. Performed at the Fourth *Cumbre Flamenca*, Madrid 1986.

'**La del Pipa, Tía Juana**' –D– (Juana de los Reyes Valencia), Jerez de la Frontera (Cadiz) 1905–1987. Daughter of *cantaor* **Luis 'el de La Maora'**. Her first husband was a street-seller of sunflower seeds (*pipas*), whence her nickname. Her second marriage, to dancer '**El Bizco Guzi**', produced singer **Juana Fernández** and dancer **Antonio 'El Pipa'**. First danced in public at the age of fourteen, at an homage to '**Tío Parrilla**'. Came to the attention of **Antonio 'Mairena'**. Performed at the Cordoba competition, then at *Las Cuevas de Nerja*, a Madrid *tablao*, with a group of veterans from the province of Cadiz. Went on to dance in other *tablaos* and at other festivals. Her manner of dancing the *bulería*, gathering up her flounced skirts and shaking the train, was at once personal and traditional, astonishing in its elegance and authenticity.

§'**La Piriñaca** (or **Periñaca**), **Tía Anica**' –S– (Ana Blanco Soto), Jerez de la Frontera (Cadiz) 1899-1987. Sister of 'El Enano' and 'El Gachó'. Not pure Gitano but, with some Gitano blood on her father's side, what the Jerez Gitanos call an *entreverá*. Never sang until she was widowed, in the early 1950s. Performed primarily at *peñas* and some festivals. Her reminiscences were collected by José Luis Ortiz Nuevo and published as *Yo tenía mu güena estrella* ('I Had a Very Lucky Star'). An excellent interpreter of *soleares* and of the *siguiriyas* of **'Tío José de Paola'**.

'El Piyayo' –S, G– (Rafael Flores Nieto), Malaga 1864-1940. Spent part of his youth in Cuba, probably during the War of Independence. Created very distinctive *tangos* with clear Latin American influences, which were also much in evidence in his interpretations of *carceleras** and *romances*.

'El Planeta' –S, G– (?), Cadiz eighteenth-nineteenth century. A legendary singer of whom little is known save that he interpreted *romances, serranas**, *polos* and *siguiriyas*, and that he was mentor to **'El Fillo'** and **'María Borrico'**. A *siguiriya cabal* attributed to him has been passed on to us by **Pepe 'Torre'**.

'El Polaco' –S– (Luis Heredia Fernández), b. Grenada 1950. Made his début in the *zambras* of Sacromonte, going on to accompany dancers like **Mario Maya**, **'Manolete'** and **'Mariquilla'** and to take part in shows like *Macama jonda, ¡Ay! Jondo, Diquela de la Alhambra* and *El Sacromonte y yo*. A very accomplished singer who has won numerous awards.

'Porrinas de Badajoz' –S– (José Salazar Molina), b. Badajoz 1924, d. Madrid 1977. Sang from childhood while working as a shoe-shine boy, made his first public appearance in 1934 at Valverde de Leganés. His real popularity dates from 1952, when he replaced **Rafael 'Farina'** in *La copla andaluza* at Madrid's *Pavón* theatre. One evening, at a party at the home of the Marquis of Villaverde, his companions generously conferred upon him the title 'Marquis de Porrinas', of which he was extremely proud. At his best when performing *fandangos* and the *jaleos* and *tangos* of his native Estremadura.

'El Potito' –S– (Antonio Vargas Cortés), b. Seville 1976. Son of singer/dancer/guitarist **'Changuito'**. From earliest childhood sang in the streets of Seville, where he was discovered by **'Pepe de Lucía'**. Thanks to his sense of rhythm and a prodigious voice capable of hitting incredibly high notes, was an overnight sensation in the world of flamenco. His brilliant career hit some snags around the time his voice was breaking, but soon got back on track. Performed at the New Musical Seminar, New York 1992, took part in Carlos Saura's 1995 film *Flamenco*, and has recorded with Jorge Pardo.

'El Príncipe Gitano' –S, D– (Enrique Castellón Vargas), b. Valencia 1932. Brother of **Dolores Vargas 'La Terremoto'**. Alternated between flamenco and bullfighting from the very beginning of his career. Later achieved fame as a singer in the *aflamencado* style and as an actor. Formed his first company in 1949 and travelled to Latin America with *Rumbo español*, the first of a long series of shows with which he toured Europe and the Americas. In the genre of flamenco *senso stricto,* his talents were put to best use in *fandangos* and *festero* styles.

'Rancapino' –S– (Alonso Núñez Núñez), b. Chiclana de la Frontera (Cadiz) 1945. Began his singing career alongside **'Camarón'** at private sesions at the *Venta de Vargas*. Went on to sing in Madrid *tablaos,* tour abroad (in France and Japan), and perform in numerous festivals. A very good interpreter of *soleares, siguiriyas* and **'El Mellizo'**'s *malagueñas*.

'La Repompa' –S– (Enriqueta Reyes Porras), Malaga 1937-1959. Sister of **Rafaela 'La Repompilla'**. Made her professional début at a very early age in the taverns of the *El Perchel* and *La Trinidad* quarters of her native city before joining flamenco group *Los Vargas* and going on to perform in the *tablaos* and theatres of Malaga, Seville, Palamós (Catalonia), Madrid and San Sebastián. Despite her untimely death from peritonitis, she is remembered as a very original performer. Recreated the *tangos* of Malaga, which she inherited from **'La Pirula'**.

'La del Revuelo', Juana –S, D– Juana Silva Esteban), b. Seville 1952. Wife of **Martín 'El del Revuelo'**. Began her career in the *tablaos,* first of Seville and then of Madrid, going on to perform in festivals and give concerts in *peñas*. Recorded an album entitled *A Compás* in 1994. An excellent *festera* dancer and singer, often appears on stage with a basket in her hand; her art is full of fresh good humour.

'Romerito de Jerez' (**'Cipote'**) –S– (Manuel Romero Pantoja), b. Jerez de la Frontera (Cadiz) 1932. Brother of **'El Guapo'**. Sang and danced in bars at a very early age in the company of **'Terremoto',** with whom he made his professional début at Seville's *El Guajiro tablao.* Joined **'Imperio de Triana'**'s company, then went back to performing in *tablaos* in Seville and Madrid, supplemented with numerous festival and concert appearances. A good sense of *compás*, extensive knowledge of all styles, and a voice at once sweet and *flamenco* are his main characteristics.

'Rubichi' –S– (Diego de los Santos Bermúdez), b. Jerez de la Frontera (Cadiz) 1949. Son of *cantaor* **Diego 'Rubichi'** and cousin of **'El**

Agujetas'. Started off in **Manuel Morao**'s 'Flamenco Thursdays' and went on to take part in many festivals and competitions. A great connoisseur of the styles of Jerez, excels at *martinetes, siguiriyas, soleares* and *saetas*.

'Sabina', María –S– (María Macías Moreno), Cadiz 189?–1979. Wife of **'Seis Reales'** and mother of **Santiago 'Donday'**. Sang only at intimate gatherings, but her deep, original singing style overflowing with *compás* has come down to us thanks to a couple of rare recordings (*Rito y Geografía del cante, Historia del Flamenco*).

'Sabicas' –G– (Agustín Castellón Campos), b. Pamplona 1912, d. New York 1990. A self-taught guitarist who first performed in public at the age of seven in his native Pamplona; within three years had established himself at Madrid's *El Dorado* theatre, also taking part in flamenco sessions at the *Villa Rosa*. Toured extensively from 1920–1930, travelled to America with **Carmen Amaya** in 1936, moved to Mexico in 1950 and lived there until finally settling in New York in 1955. From 1967 until his death in 1990 made frequent visits to Spain to perform in homages, concerts and various shows. Shortly before he died, recorded eighteen tracks with **Enrique Morente**. His sound was very distinctive, a dazzling virtuosity that never descended into mere technicality, a wonderful alliance of skill and *duende*.

Salazar, José –S– (José Salazar Salazar), b. Badajoz 1941. Husband of **'La Caleta'**. Lived at Huelva from earliest childhood and made his début there at the age of ten. Joined **Concha Piquer**'s company in 1955 and won many prizes at the Cordoba competition the following year. Performed in many of Madrid's *tablaos* and toured abroad – Japan, America and Europe – particularly with **Antonio 'Gades'**. An admirer of the work of **Antonio 'Mairena'**, excels at classic styles and *tarantos*.

'La Serneta' –S– (Merced Fernández Vargas), b. Jerez de la Frontera (Cadiz) 1834, d. Utrera (Seville) 1912. Little is known about this great singer, apart from the fact that she lived in Utrera most of her life, gave guitar lessons to some of Madrid's aristocratic families, and enjoyed enormous prestige among the professional singers of her day. Composed at least seven *soleares* which have been passed on by **Chacón**, **'Manuel Torre'**, **Tomás** and **Pastora Pavón**, and **'Vallejo'**, among others.

'Sernita de Jerez' –S– (Manuel Fernández Moreno), b. Jerez de la Frontera (Cadiz) 1921, d. Madrid 1971. A descendant of **'Joaquín**

Lacherna', nephew of **'El Tati'** and of **'Juanichi El Manijero'**, father of guitarist **'Curro de Jerez'** and of the dancer **'Manuela La Serna'**. Made his first public appearance in 1935 at the *Teatro Eslava* in Jerez, followed by many years in which he sang only at private gatherings. In 1957 came back into the public eye, touring and performing in *tablaos*. A member of **Antonio**'s troupe, with which he toured the world from 1962 to 1969. A singer with a vast repertoire, recognised as one of the masters of Jerez styles.

'Serranito' –G– (Victor Monge Serrano), b. Madrid 1942. Began his professional career at twelve when he toured America with *Los Chavalillos de España*, followed by tours with **Juanito Valderrama** and **Lucero Tena**. Also performed in numerous Madrid *tablaos* before undertaking a solo career which brought him great success in Australia, New Zealand, Africa and America. Among his more remarkable concerts were one at London's Queen Elizabeth Hall and another for the BBC, not to mention others in Tokyo, Paris, New York and Moscow. His 1983 tour of the United States was particularly noteworthy, as was his celebration concert in Strasbourg on the occasion of Spain's entry to the Council of Europe, the 1991 presentation of his *Ecos del Guadalquivir* at New York's Metropolitan Opera House, and his *Huellas...* at *La Maestranza* in Seville, 1998. A virtuoso guitarist, yet faithful to tradition and very inspired.

'La Singla' –D– (Antonia Singla Contreras), b. Barcelona 1948. Started off in Catalonia and in the *tablaos* of Madrid. Took part in the 1963 film *Los Tarantos* with **Carmen Amaya**. In 1968, following her cure from deafness, she set up a group of her own and made numerous tours abroad with a show entitled *Festival flamenco gitano*.

'El Sordera' –S– (Manuel Soto Monje), b. Jerez de la Frontera (Cadiz) 1927. A descendant of **'Paco La Luz'**, nephew of **'La Serrana'**, **'La Sordida'**, and **'Tío José de Paola'**, father of **Vicente** and **José Soto**. Started his career in the *Plata y Oro* café in Jerez, where he sang until 1944. The following year he won a prize for his *saetas*. In 1953, performed at *El Guajiro*, a Seville *tablao*, followed by international tours with **María Rosa** and **Manuela Vargas**, and by appearances in Madrid *tablaos*, and at *peñas* and festivals. Recognised as a master of the Jerez styles: *siguiriyas, soleares*, **'El Gloria'**'s *fandangos*, and *bulerías*. His singing is vibrant and emotional, characterised by uncontrollable shuddering.

'Talega', Juan –S– (Juan Agustín Fernández Vargas), Dos Hermanas (Seville) 1891-1971. Son of **Agustín 'Talega'** and nephew of **Joaquín 'el de La Paula'**. A cattle merchant who only sang at private gatherings until the 1950s, when **Antonio 'Mairena'** coaxed him into performing in public. His *tonás*, *siguiriyas* and *soleares* won him first prize at the 1959 Cordoba competition, after which he took part in many festivals. Considered a grand master of the songs of Alcalá, passed down from his father and uncle.

'Terremoto (de Jerez)' –D, S– (Fernando Fernández Monje), Jerez de la Frontera (Cadiz) 1936–1981. Started off as a dancer in and around Jerez, followed by a stint at Seville's *El Guajiro tablao*. Did not sing professionally until the 1950s, at first in taverns, then in *tablaos* in Seville, Barcelona and Madrid where, in the late 1960s, he became lead singer with *Las Brujas*. The most *flamenco* and, all in all, the greatest singer of his time. His voice, with its cracked, *afillá* quality, and his unique *duende*, could not fail to incite *pellizco**.

'Terremoto', Fernando ('Terremoto Hijo') –S– (Fernando Fernández Pantoja), b. Jerez de la Frontera (Cadiz) 1970. Son of **'Terremoto de Jerez'**, started off as a guitarist but at the age of twenty suddenly decided to take up singing and surprised audiences with the echo in his voice, very close to that of his father whose style he carries on.

'Tomasa, José el de La' –S– (José Georgio Soto), b. Seville 1951. Grandson of **Pepe 'Torre'**, son of singer **'Tomasa'** and **'Pies de Plomo'**. Won the **Manuel 'Torre'** prize at the 1976 Cordoba competition, after which he took to performing in *peñas* and festivals. Worthy heir to a glorious family tradition, he is also the author of *letras flamencas** (lyrics), a collection of which was published in 1990 under the title *Alma de barco*.

'Tomatito' –G– (José Fernández Torres), b. Almería 1958. Performed in public from a very young age in his native town before becoming accompanist to **'Camarón'**, with whom he recorded half a dozen albums between 1981 and 1992. Has accompanied many other singers, among them **Enrique Morente**, **Vicente Soto**, and **'Luis de Córdoba'**. His brilliant, very *flamenco* playing style has won him many followers among young guitarists.

'Torre', Manuel –S– (Manuel Soto Loreto), b. Jerez de la Frontera (Cadiz) 1878, d. Seville 1933. Son of **Juan 'Torre'** and nephew of **Joaquín 'Lacherna'**. Started off in the *cafés cantantes* of Jerez, moving on to those of Seville in 1902; also performed in Madrid and Barcelona. Took part in the 1922 Grenada competition as an invited artist, and later toured with various shows organised by Vedrines and known collectively as *ópera flamenca*. Many tales are told of **Manuel 'Torre'**'s eccentricities, his greyhounds and fighting cocks. A manic, unpredictable personality, one never knew how he would sing or even if he would do so. Yet when he was possessed by the *duende* his singing had spectacular, trance-inducing effects; carried away in their delirious enthusiasm, listeners threw chairs and tore their clothing. His *saetas* were like arrows and his *siguiriyas* gouged like a knifeblade.

'Torre', Tomás –S, D– (Tomás Soto Lahera), b. Jerez de la Frontera (Cadiz) 1929. Note that three different artists bore the name **Tomás 'Torre'**. There was **Tomás Soto Torres**, son of **Manuel** and **'La Gamba'** who died in 1976; second, **Tomás Soto Reyes**, nephew of **Manuel** and **Pepe 'Torre'**, who died in 1955; and third, his son and nephew of **'La Tomasa'**, **Tomás Soto Lahera**, a *festero* artist who has performed in many shows and festivals and to whom the *Cátedra* awarded its *Copa Jerez* in 1976.

'El Torta' –S– (Juan Moneo Lara), b. Jerez de la Frontera (Cadiz) 1952. Brother of **Manuel Moneo**, nephew of **'Luis de Pacote'** and **'El Chico'**. Some *tablao* work but more associated with festivals and *peñas*. Influenced by such diverse sources as **'Agujetas'**, **'Camarón'** and **Antonio 'Mairena'**, has forged a very personal style with great emotional impact. Excels at *soleares* and *bulerías*.

'Tragapanes' –S– (José Rodríguez Lara), b. Seville 1908. Grandson of **'Cagancho'** and of the matador 'Chicorro'. Born in Triana, performed exclusively at private gatherings until taking part in the 1985 show *Los últimos de la fiesta*. Performed at the Third *Cumbre Flamenca* in Madrid, 1985.

Vargas, Angelita ('La Gitanilla') –D– (Angelita Vargas Vega), b. Seville 1949. Married to **'El Biencasao'** and mother of dancer **'Joselito'** (José Cortés Vargas). Performed at *Los Gallos*, a Seville *tablao*. In 1980 won the *Pastora Imperio* prize at the Cordoba competition and became one of the greatest stars of the Andalusian festival scene, usually accompanied by her husband and son. Her style, at once traditional in its attitudes and modern in its *compás*, is profoundly *flamenco*.

Vargas, Aurora –S, D– (Aurora Vargas Vargas), b. Seville 1956. Made her stage début in Japan alongside her husband, the singer **'Jarillo'**, then went on to appear in Seville *tablaos* and at festivals. Enjoyed remarkable success at Seville's 1974 Flamenco Fortnight; took part in the Third Biennial in the Andalusian capital, in 1984, Madrid's *Cumbre Flamenca* and the Fourth *Noches de Andalucía*, Oloron, both in 1986, and, in 1988, in the show accompanying the first international *Dos siglos de flamenco* conference, in Jerez. A real force of nature, superbly fierce in her dance, tender and passionate in song. Her 'ripped' voice gives the best of its *duende* when she is on the brink of exhaustion.

Vargas, Concha –D– (Concepción Vargas Torres), b. Lebrija (Seville) 1956. Having spent some time at *El café de Chinitas* in Madrid in the early 1970s, moved on to the *tablaos* of Seville and took part in many tours abroad and in numerous flamenco shows including *Camelamos Naquerar* with **Mario Maya**'s troupe, *Diálogos con Dios* with **Curro Fernández** and *Persecución* with **'El Lebrijano'**. Toured France with **Pedro 'Bacan'** and *Le Clan des Pinini*, 1989, and took part in the 1992 show *Nuestra historia al sur*.

Vargas, Manolo –S– (Manuel Vargas Gómez), b. Cadiz 1907, d. Madrid 1970. After touring with **'Mariemma'**'s troupe, sang at the *Zambra* and later at the *Villa Rosa*, both in Madrid. Specialised in the songs of Cadiz, which he interpreted with passion and a remarkable sense of rhythm.

Vargas, María –S– (María Vargas Fernández), b. Sanlúcar de Barrameda (Cadiz) 1947. Made her début very young, accompanied by **'Manolo Sanlúcar':** her first appearance at the *Teatro Villamarta* in Jerez, when she was just twelve, caused a sensation. Went on to perform in various Madrid *tablaos*. Received the title 'Queen of the *Primeros Juegos Florales del Flamenco*', 1969, and was awarded the *Copa Jerez* by the *Cátedra de Flamencología* the same year. Possesses a vast repertoire and is particularly distinguished in her singing of *festeros* songs.

Vega, Alejandro –S– (Alejandro Vega Arincón), b. Badajoz 1960. A cousin of **'Porrinas'** and uncle of **Remedios Amaya**. Excels in the styles of Estremadura, particularly the *jaleos*.

Villar, Juanito –S– (Juan José Villar Jiménez), b. Cadiz 1947. Son of **'La Jineta'**, nephew of **'El Jineto'** and of **'Pablito de Cadiz'**. Made his début aged seven in the group *Los Chavalillos Gaditanos*. His absolute mastery of *compás* meant that he was much in demand as a dance accompanist, with the likes of **'La Tati'**, **Manuela Carrasco**, **'Faico'** and **'El Güito'**. Performed in many of Madrid's *tablaos* and made numerous tours abroad before switching, in the 1970s, to festivals in Andalusia. One of the greatest living masters of the styles of Cadiz.

'El Yunque' –S– (Ricardo Losada Maya), b. Madrid 1946. Uncle of guitarist **Felipe Maya**. Made his début at fifteen in the show *Paso a la juventud* at Madrid's *Circo Price*, subsequently performed in many of the capital's *tablaos*. Awarded the *Granaínas* Prize at the 1983 Cordoba competition and took part in the Madrid *Cumbre Flamenca*, 1985. A very accomplished singer, particularly gifted in the interpretation of 'free' (*libres*) songs.

Sources:

Personal memories and archives

Flamenco journals: *Candil, La Caña, El Olivo, Sevilla Flamenca*

Pedro Calvo, José Manuel Gamboa, *Historia-Guia del Nuevo Flamenco* (Madrid, 1994)

Luis Soler Guevara & Ramón Soler Díaz, *Antonio Mairena en el mundo de la siguiriya y la soleá* (Malaga, 1992)

Luis Soler Guevara & Ramón Soler Díaz, *Historia del Flamenco: 'Testimonios Flamencos'* (Seville, 1996)

Pierre Lefranc, *Le Cante Jondo* (Nice, 1998)

Fernando el de Triana, *Arte y Artistas flamencos* (Cordoba, 1978)

José Blas Vega & Manuel Ríos Ruiz, *Diccionario enciclopédico ilustrado del Flamenco* (Madrid, 1988)

Glossary

Aficionado – A fan, especially of flamenco or bullfighting.

Afillá – A raucous, very Gitano voice, such as that of Francisco Ortega Vargas 'El Fillo'.

Aflamencado/a – Said of a tune or song that has been influenced by flamenco, or which is interpreted in a flamenco manner.

Alboreá – A Gitano wedding song. In principle, **alboreás** are avoided on other occasions, as singing them out of context is said to bring bad luck.

Alcalde – The principal administrative and judicial officer in a municipality or district.

Alegrías – Songs from the **cantiñas** group, typical of Cadiz.

Arabo-Andalusian – Adjective applied to the art, and in particular to the poetry and music, of the Andalusian Arabs, certain forms of which survive in North Africa.

Arsenal – Naval dockyard where military ships are built, repaired, fitted and armed.

Bailaor/a – A dancer of flamenco or folk dances, as opposed to *balairín/a,* a dancer of classical or modern dance.

Bamberas – Songs to accompany young girls swinging on giant swings – *bambas* – at certain festivals.

Betica – Name of a Roman province in the south of the Iberian peninsula, approximately corresponding to modern Andalusia. The phrase 'Betica Gitanos' is used by certain Spanish authors claiming a different origin for Andalusian Gitanos than for those elsewhere, and also stipulating that this group arrived in the peninsula long before the fifteenth century. The hypothesis has no scientific foundation.

Bögö (or **szaj bögö** – 'bass vocal') – Term borrowed from Hungarian to designate a technique used by Rom of the Wallachian (*Vlax*) group for their dance music (**khelimaski gili**) and which consists in marking the rhythm – both beat and off-beat – with the aid of various sounds produced by the mouth.

Buleaeros – Artists who specialise in **bulerías**.

Bulerías – Song and dance performed to a very fast rhythm derived from that of the **soleá**. Those of Jerez are particularly highly esteemed.

Bulería por soleá – An intermediate rhythm, halfway between that of the **bulería** and the **soleá.**

Byzantines – The Byzantines occupied part of Andalusia from 554–629. There is no evidence that this occupation had any influence on the region's music, but posterity has tended to confuse the primitive Hispanic liturgy (sometimes mistakenly called **Mozarabic**) with the Byzantine liturgy.

Cabal – A type of **siguiriya** in a major key, sung as a transition (**cambio**) or finale (*remate*).

Cafés cantantes or **de cante** – Establishments offering musical entertainment, including flamenco, that sprang up around the mid-nineteenth century.

Caló – Literally, 'black'. **Gitanos'** own name for themselves and their language.

Cambio – A song used as a form of transition.

Caña – A type of song related to the **soleá**, with the repetition of a vowel as refrain.

Cantaor/a – A flamenco singer, as opposed to a *cantante* (singer of other types of songs).

Cante – Andalusian form of the word *canto* (song), used as a synonym for flamenco song.

Cante jondo – In Andalusian dialect, 'deep song'. A euphemism proposed by Manuel de Falla and Federico García Lorca to replace the term 'flamenco', which had acquired deeply pejorative overtones at the time (early twentieth century).

Cantiñas – A family of songs originating in Cadiz, among them the *alegrías*, *caracoles*, *mirabrás* and *romeras*.

Carcelera – A song from the **tonás** group, in which the lyrics usually refer to prison (*carcela*).

Catholic Monarchs – Fernando II of Aragon (reigned 1474–1516) and Isabel I of Castile (reigned 1474–1504), better known in English as Ferdinand and Isabella. Their marriage achieved political unity for Spain. They went on to reconquer the last bastion of Islamic rule, **Grenada**.

Charles I (1500–1558) – King of Spain under this title. Also Emperor of Germany as Charles V and King of Sicily as Charles IV.

Colmao – A bar/restaurant where **aficionados** gathered to watch more or less spontaneous flamenco performances when the **cafés cantantes** declined.

Compás – Spanish for (musical) beat. In flamenco terminology, designates the rhythm specific to a given type of song.

Copla – Any type of verse to be sung. Flamenco **coplas** are usually self-contained units with regard to meaning.

Corregidor – Judicial magistrate and supreme local authority in certain large cities.

Cortes, Las – An assembly comprising representatives of the 'states' (that is,

social classes – whence its other name, **States General**) and the cities, con-
vened by the king for the purpose of advising on certain aspects of government (power remained firmly with the monarch) and particularly to authorise
the levying of certain exceptional taxes.

Council (*Consejo de Castilla*) – A body which acted as supreme tribunal and as
consultant to the monarch.

Duende – A state of exaltation or trance brought about by flamenco music. Also
used to describe a flamenco artist's ability to evoke this in others.

Etudes Tsiganes ('Gypsy Studies') – Association founded in Paris in the 1950s
and also the title of its scholarly journal.

Fandango – A type of folksong that has often been drawn towards flamenco.

Festero – Lighthearted song or dance suited to festive occasions.

Flamenco – A song, music and dance genre. Also used more broadly, to designate a type of voice or interpretation, and in connection with individuals who
embody the lifestyle and philosophy whence the music springs. Italicised in
the text when used in this latter sense.

Galleys – Manpower at the oars remained an essential adjunct to wind power
until both were eventually replaced by steam. Able-bodied male convicts
were frequently sentenced to this form of hard labour, which was often a
death sentence.

Garrotín – A type of dance. Some claim it originated in Asturia, others ascribe it
to the Gitanos of Lérida. The song accompanying it has become 'flamenco'
thanks to 'La Niña de los Peines'.

'Generation of '98' – A group of writers of this era, known *inter alia* for their
anti-flamenco stance. In 1922, de Falla, García Lorca and others organised
the first flamenco competition as a counter-move, to rehabilitate this music.

Ghawazi – The dancing girls, usually Gypsy, of Egypt.

Gitano/s (noun and adjective) – The Gypsies of Spain and Southern France, who
call themselves **Caló.**

Granaína – A song of the **fandango** group; according to some, originally part of
the folklore of the Grenada region, according to others, a creation of Antonio
Chacón's.

Grenada, reconquest of – The *Reconquista* (reconquest of Spain by indigenous
Spaniards) was a gradual process over a period of centuries. Grenada, the
final bastion, was re-taken in 1492 under the **Catholic Monarchs**, thus
ending seven centuries of Islamic rule in Spain.

Guardia Civil – Military corps for the pursuit of outlaws in rural areas, set up in
1844 to replace the old **Santa Hermandad.**

Iglesias frías – The right of an individual claiming sanctuary (ecclesiastical
immunity from the secular authorities) on Church property to remain under
Church protection even after being forcibly removed from such property.
Until repealed in 1748, this law meant that, after trial, the accused had to be

returned to the premises from which he had been arrested.

Jaleo – A type of song from Estremadura, related to the **bulería.**

Jarcha – See **Kharja.**

Jondo – In Andalusian dialect, 'deep'. See **Cante jondo.**

Juergas – Intimate get-togethers of flamenco artists and **aficionados** (akin to 'sessions' in jazz circles).

Kharja (noun, singular and plural) – Final stanza of the Arabo-Andalusian poetic form known as **muwashshah**, usually borrowed from popular verse, sometimes in the **Mozarabic** language.

Khelimaski gili – see **Bögö.**

Latifundia (sg. **latifundium**) – Vast agricultural estates, worked extensively and by archaic methods.

Letra – The text of a **copla**: song lyrics.

Liviana – A type of song similar to the **serrana**, related to the **siguiriya** by its rhythm but easier to perform.

Malagueña – A type of song derived from a **fandango** of the Malaga region, transformed into the flamenco genre in the early nineteenth century.

Martinete – Song from the **tonás** group, generally associated with work at the anvil.

Minera – Song from the Levante, the lyrics of which usually refer to work in the mines.

Mozarab – Historically, pertaining to indigenous Christians living in Muslim-dominated regions of Spain. Adjectival form, **Mozarabic**, used to describe their language and music.

Muwashshah – An Arabic poem composed to be set to music, terminating in a folk-style couplet or refrain in the vernacular (**jarcha** or **kharja**).

Nana – A lullaby.

New Castilian – Expression coined in the eighteenth century to replace the word 'Gypsy' when this was banned by law, in contrast to **Old Castilian** (a person of Spanish stock). Based on the model of the term *New Christian*, formerly applied to converted Jews and Muslims *(Conversos)* as opposed to indigenous Christians or persons of Spanish stock, called *Old Christians*.

Old Castilian – Expression coined in the eighteenth century to designate persons of Spanish stock, as distinct from **New Castilian**, the compulsory neologism for 'Gypsy'.

Ópera flamenca – Touring shows, usually put together by a professional producer/manager. Had their heyday in the 1920s and 1930s.

Pandas – Small folk orchestras that play **fandangos** known as **verdiales.**

Payo/a (noun and adjective) – (A) non-Gypsy.

Pellizco – Literally 'tightening': the emotion produced by a singer who possesses the **duende.**

Peña – Club specialising in flamenco, set up by **aficionados.**

Petenera – Type of song attributed to a singer from Paterna de Ribera (Cadiz), its most highly developed form is a creation of 'La Niña de los Peines'.

Polo – A type of song related to the **caña.**

Pragmatic (Sp. *Real Pragmática*) – A type of decree, signed by the Monarch.

Privilege – Document entitling the holder to exemption from some current legislation, for example, exempting a Gypsy from general anti-Gypsy measures.

Rajo – A 'ripped' quality peculiar to certain singing voices, particularly Gitano ones.

Romance – A narrative ballad in octosyllabic verses.

Romungro – The word used by Rom of the Wallachian (*Vlax)* group to designate sedentary 'Hungarian' groups, from whom professional musicians are drawn.

Rumba – Type of song and dance of Cuban origin. Very popular in Spain in the first half of the twentieth century.

Saeta – Folk song on a religious theme, performed during Holy Week processions, adapted to flamenco under the influence of **tonás** and **siguiriyas.**

Santa Hermandad ('Holy Brotherhood') – Militia established in 1476 by the **Catholic Monarchs** for the pursuit of outlaws in rural areas.

Serrana – A type of song with the same rhythmic structure as the **siguiriya** but distinguished by its melody and characteristic lyrics.

Siguiriya or **seguiriya** – One of the basic song styles of flamenco, characterised by twelve-beat rhythmic/melodic sequences.

Soleá (plural: **soleares**) – One of the basic song styles of flamenco. Like the **siguiriya**, characterised by twelve-beat rhythm.

Soleá por bulería –A quick-tempo **soleá**, closer to a **bulería.**

States General – see **Las Cortes.**

Tablao – Cabaret specialising in flamenco shows, modelled on the old **cafés cantantes**. Came into existence in the 1950s.

Tango – A dance of African origin further developed in Latin America before becoming popular in Spain around the middle of the nineteenth century. The Gitanos quickly adapted it to the flamenco repertoire.

Taranto – A danceable variety of the *taranta*, a type of song from the Levante region.

Tientos – A variety of **tango** performed to a slower tempo.

Tonás – Unaccompanied songs, considered, along with the **romances**, to be among the most ancient in the flamenco repertoire.

Venta – A country inn.

Verdiales – A type of **fandango** from the Malaga region.

Villancico – A traditional Christmas carol.

Zambra – A show from Grenada's Sacromonte, based on Gitano wedding rituals. The term is also used to describe a type of **aflamencado** song made fashionable by 'Manolo Caracol' and Lola Flores.

Select bibliography

Alvarez Caballero, Angel, *Historia del cante flamenco* (Madrid, 1981)

Andrade de Silva, Tomás, 'Sur les origines de trente-trois cantes' in *Anthologie du Cante flamenco* (Paris, 1954)

Barkechli, Mehdi, 'La musique iranienne' in *Histoire de la Musique* (Paris, 1960)

Barrios, Manuel, *Proceso al gitanismo* (Seville, 1980)

Barrios, Manuel, *Gitanos, Moriscos y cante flamenco* (Seville, 1989)

Barrios, Manuel, 'Sobre el gratuito invento del cante gitano' in *Candil No 83,* Sept-Oct 1992

Blas Vega, José, and Rios Ruiz, Manuel, *Diccionario enciclopédico ilustrado del Flamenco* (Madrid, 1988)

Camacho Galindo, Pedro, *Los payos también cantan flamenco* (Madrid, 1975)

Cervantes, Miguel de, 'La Gitanilla' in *Novelas ejemplares* (many editions)

Davanellos, Nick, 'Les Tsiganes et la musique démotique grecque' in *Tsiganes: Identité, Evolution* (Paris, 1989)

Estebanez Calderón, Serafin, *Escenas andaluzas* (Buenos Aires, 1941)

Falla, Manuel de, *Escritos sobre mùsica y mùsicos* (Buenos Aires, 1950)

Garcia Lorca, Federico, 'El cante jondo', 'Teorìa y juego del duende', 'Arquitectura del cante jondo', and 'Poema del cante jondo' in *Obras completas* (many editions)

Garcia Matos, Manuel, *Sobre el Flamenco: estudios y notas* (Madrid, 1984)

Gomez Alfaro, Antonio, *The Great Gypsy Round-up* (Madrid, 1993)

Gonzalez, Norma, 'De los gitanos de Flandes a los gitanos flamencos' in *Candil No 24,* Nov-Dec 1982

Grande, Félix, *Memoria del Flamenco* (Madrid, 1979)

Hadju, André, 'Le Folklore tsigane' in *Etudes Tsiganes* (Paris, 1962)

Larrea Palacin, Arcadio, *El flamenco en su raíz* (Madrid, 1974)

Leblon, Bernard, *Les Gitans dans la littérature espagnole* (Toulouse, 1982)

Leblon, Bernard, *Les Gitans d'Espagne* (Paris, 1985)

Leblon, Bernard, *Los gitanos de España: el precio y el valor de la differencia* (Barcelona, 1987)

Leblon, Bernard, *Musiques tsiganes et Flamenco* (Paris, 1990)

Leblon, Bernard, *El cante flamenco, entre las mùsicas gitanas y las tradiciones andaluzas* (Madrid, 1991)

Luna, José Carlos de, *Gitanos de la Bética* (Madrid, 1951)

Mata Carriazo, Juan de, *Hechos del Condestable don Miguel Lucas de Iranzo* (Madrid, 1940)

Medina Azara, 'Cante jondo y cantares sinagogales' in *Revista de Occidente* (Madrid, 1930)

Mercado, José, *La seguidilla gitana* (Madrid, 1982)

Molina, Ricardo, and Mairena, Antonio, 'Mundo y formas del cante flamenco' in *Revista de Occidente* (Madrid, 1963)

Munoz, Eusebia, *Voces flamencas* (Perpignan, 1982)

Ortiz de Villajos, Candido G., *Gitanos de Granada: la zambra* (Granada, 1949)

Pedrell, Felipe, *Cancionero musical popular español* (Valls, 1918-1922)

Ropero Nuñez, *El léxico caló en el lenguaje del cante flamenco* (Seville, 1984)

Rossy, Hipólito, *Teoría del cante jondo* (Barcelona, 1966)

Swinburne, Henry, *Travels Through Spain* (London, 1779)

Vallecillo, Francisco, *Antonio Mairena, la pequeña historia* (Jerez, 1988)

Vaux de Foletier, François de, *Mille Ans d'Histoire des Tsiganes* (Paris, 1970)

Weber, Alain, 'Les Tsiganes d'Egypte' in *Etudes Tsiganes* (Paris, 1989)

Select discography

This is a highly selective list of classic recordings, most of which are available from specialist outlets.

Collections

Magna Antología del Cante Flamenco (10 CD set + 86-page book). Madrid, Hispavox, 1982, S/C. 66.201.

Testimonios Flamencos (40 CD set + 2-volume *Historia del Flamenco*). Seville, Tartessos, 1996.

Medio Siglo de Cante Flamenco (71 songs on 4 CDs + booklet). Madrid, Ariola Eurodisc, 1987.

El Cante Flamenco 'Antología Histórica' (57 songs on 3 CDs + booklet). Madrid, Polygram Iberica (Philips), 1987.

Artists (in chronological order)

Manuel Torre: *Grabaciones históricas 1909-1931* (2 CD set).

La Niña de los Peines: *Voz de Estaño Fundido* (1 CD, 24 songs, 1910-1950).

Niño Caracol: *Primeras Grabaciones realizadas en 1930* (1 CD). Seville, Pasarela, 1997.

Antonio Mairena: *Grabaciones Completas, 197 Cantes* (16 CD set + booklet). Madrid, Cinterco, 1995.

Pedro Bacán et les Pinini: *Noches Gitanas en Lebrija* (4 CD set). Paris, EPM, 1991.

Camarón: *Antología* (54 songs on 3 CD set + booklet).

Manuel Morao y Gitanos de Jerez: *Bulerías en Compás de Origen* (1 CD). Jerez, Gitanos de Jerez, 1997.

La Macanita: *Jerez, Xères, Sherry* (1 CD). Madrid, Nuevos Medios, 1998.

Videos

Francisco Rovira Beleta: *Los Tarantos* (with Carmen Amaya, Antonio Gades, Peret, La Singla etc.). Barcelona, Manga Films, 1963.

Carlos Saura: *Flamenco* (Mario Maya, José Mercé, Chocolate, Manuela Carrasco, Farruco, Fernanda de Utrera, La Paquera, Agujeta, Aurora Vargas, La Macanita, Rancapino, Tomatito, Duquende etc.). Seville, Juan Lebron, 1995.

Carmen Amaya (Especial Coleccionistas): *Gipsy Dance* (Hollywood 1941) and *Embrujo del Flamenco* (Cuba 1937).

Rito y Geografía del Cante, Murcia, Alga, 1997. (Filmed between 1971–1973, this set of 26 videos, with an accompanying book, features the greatest flamenco artists of the time.)

Flamenco books, CDs and videos are available by post from:

El Mundo Flamenco, 62 Duke St, London W1K 6JT
   www.elmundoflamenco.com
   tel 020 7493 0033
   fax 020 7495 4610

El Flamenco Vive, Conde de Lemos 7, 28013 Madrid, Spain
   www.elflamencovive.es
   tel 0034 91 547 3917
   fax 0034 91 542 1639

The *Interface Collection*

The *Interface Collection* was developed by the Centre for Gypsy Research at the Université René Descartes in Paris in association with publishers throughout Europe and with the support of the European Commission and the Council for Europe. The Centre for Gypsy Research is at the hub of a unique international publishing programme with volumes appearing in up to twelve European languages.

This has been severely curtailed since 2001 by the loss of EU funding for the work of the specialist editorial committees and for the translations organised by the Centre for Gypsy Research and as a result only those volumes which the publishers consider to be commercially viable can now be published. This at present excludes the concluding two volumes in the important series on the Gypsies during the Second World War and further volumes in the series on the Romani language.

For further details about the work of the Centre for Gypsy Research:

Centre de recherches tsiganes
Université René Descartes
45 rue des Saints-Pères
F – 75270 - PARIS Cedex 06,
France

Tel: +33 331 42862112
Fax: +33 1 42862065
E-mail: crt@paris5.sorbonne.fr

Web address: http://www.eurrenet.com/

A list of the volumes published so far with the addresses of the publishers follows.

Titles in the *Interface Collection*

Each volume in the *Interface Collection* is published in up to twelve languages (see list of publishers). The English language editions of the *Interface Collection* are published by the University of Hertfordshire Press. Where an English language edition has not been published details of other language editions are given. The code in front of the ISBN identifies the publisher.

An updated version of this list can be seen on the web pages of the University of Hertfordshire Press at: http://www.herts.ac.uk/UHPress/interface.html

This English language edition was published outside the *Interface Collection*

Série Rukun / The Rukun Series

Eric Hill's popular *Spot the Dog* books in Romani

Publishers' addresses

ANICIA
Via San Francesco a Ripa, 62
I – 00153 – Roma , Italy
web site:
http://members.it.tripod.de/anicia

CRDP – Centre Régional de
Documentation Pédagogique
Midi-Pyrénées
3 rue Roquelaine
F – 31069 – Toulouse Cedex, France
web site: http://www.crdp-toulouse.fr

CROCUS – Vydavate°stvo CROCUS Nové
Zámky
Stefan Safranek
Bernolákovo nám. 27
SK - 940 51 - Nové Zámky
web site:
http://www.crocus.sk

EA – Editura Alternative
Casa Presei, Corp. A, Et. 6
Pia a Presei Libere, 1
RO – 71341 - Bucureşti 1, Bulgaria

EK – Editions Kastaniotis
11, Zalogou
GR – 106 78 – Athèns, Greece
web site: http://www.kastaniotis.com

HAM – Editions L'Harmattan
5-7 rue de l'Ecole Polytechnique
F – 75005 – Paris, France
web site:
http://www.editions-
harmattan.fr

IBIS – Ibis Grafika
Sasa Krnic
IV. Ravnice 25
10 000 Zagreb
Croatia
web site:
http://www.ibis-grafika.hr

LIT – Litavra
163 A – Rakovski
BG – 1000 – Sofia, Romania

PA – Edition Parabolis
Schliemannstraße 23
D – 10437 Berlin, Germany
web site: http://www.emz-berlin.de

PG – Editorial Presencia Gitana
Valderrodrigo, 76 y 78
E – 28039 – Madrid, Spain
web site:
http://www.presenciagitana.org

PONT – Pont Kiadó
Pf 215
H – 1300 Budapest 3, Hungary
web site: http://www.pontkiado.com

SE – Entreculturas / Secretariado
Coordenador dos Programas de Educação
Multicultural
Trav. das Terras de Sant'Ana, 15 – 1°
PT – 1250 – Lisboa, Portugal
web site:
http//www.min-edu.pt/entreculturas

UHP – University of Hertfordshire Press
Learning and Information Services,
College Lane – Hatfield
UK – Hertfordshire AL10 9AB, Britain
web site:
http://www.herts.ac.uk/UHPress

VUP – Univerzita Palackého v
Olomouci – Vydavatelství /
Palacky University Press
Krížkovského 8
CZ – 771 47 – Olomouc, Czech Republic

Distributor for some Rukun titles:
RB – Rromani Baxt
22, rue du Port
F – 63000 Clermont-Ferrand, France

The University of Hertfordshire Press is the only university press committed to developing a major publishing programme on social, cultural and political aspects of the Romani and other Gypsy people who migrated from north west India at the beginning of the last millennium and are now found on every continent. Recent titles include:

We are the Romani People
Ian Hancock (Interface Collection, Volume 28)
ISBN 1-902806-19-0 £9.99
An introductory guide which presents the most current findings about Romani origins, an overview of politics, culture, language and cuisine, a surprising list of notable people of Romani descent, a description of the centuries-long period of slavery in the Balkans and a brief description of the Romani Holocaust. Especially useful is the chapter on how to interact with Romanies, and the list of recommended readings. Each chapter is accompanied by a list of questions, making it suitable as a textbook for use in class.

A way of life
Donn Pohren
ISBN 1 902806 03 4 £12.95
Donn Pohren spent seven years running a flamenco centre at Morón in Andalusia, "*the wildest years of my life which I barely survived.*" *A way of life* paints an unforgettable picture of flamenco and its mainly Gypsy singers, dancers and guitarists at a time when it was still entirely genuine and part of everyday life. This new edition will introduce a new generation of flamenco enthusiasts to the spirit of flamenco and the huge contribution made to it by the Gypsies of Andalusia.
"*A way of life* will become a classic and one that is an absolute delight to read" *Guitar Review* (USA)
"A very important source to understand the history of flamenco" *Paseo* (Japan)

The Great Gypsy Roundup
Antonio Gomez Alfaro (Interface Collection, Volume 2)
ISBN 84 87347 12 6 £9.99
Translated from the original Spanish and extensively illustrated, this is the terrible story of the roundup and imprisonment of the Gypsies of Spain in 1749. Beginning with the justification for the roundup – that the Gypsies were a danger to society – the book details how the operation was carried out and the events which followed before the granting of a pardon in 1763 and the Gypsies' eventual release some two years later.

Between Past and Future: the Roma of Central and Eastern Europe
Edited by Will Guy
ISBN 1-902806-07-7 £18.99
This important new study challenges popular misconceptions, analysing how and why Roma have become victims of political and economic restructuring following the overthrow of Communist rule.

A false dawn: my life as a Gypsy woman in Slovakia
Ilona Lackova (Interface Collection, Volume 16)
ISBN 1-902806-00-X £11.99
The inspirational life story of a remarkable woman transcribed and edited from recordings in Romani. The author witnessed the destruction of the Romani culture, language and way of life in the 'false dawn' of the post-war Communist era.

What is the Romani Language?
Peter Bakker et al (Interface Collection, Volume 21)
ISBN 1-902806-06-9 £11.99
This introductory guide by an international group of specialists in the Romani language describes its origin, current use, the way it is taught and the beginnings of Romani literature and films.

The Roads of the Roma: a PEN Anthology of Gypsy writers
Edited by Ian Hancock, Siobhan Dowd and Rajko Djuric
ISBN 0-900458-90-9 £11.99
Forty-three poems and prose extracts, most appearing in English for the first time, are arranged alongside an 800-year chronology of repression. What emerges is a portrait of a people struggling to preserve their identity in a hostile world.

Shared Sorrows: a Gypsy family remembers the Holocaust
Toby Sonneman
ISBN 1-902806-10-7 £12.00
This powerful beautifully written book interweaves the story of the author's own Jewish family with that of the members of an extended family of Sinti survivors of the Holocaust which she came to know in Munich.

Gypsies under the Swastika
Donald Kenrick and Grattan Puxon (Interface Collection, Volume 8)
ISBN 0-900458-65-8 £9.99
The most comprehensive and up-to-date single-volume account of the fate of the Gypsies in the Holocaust.

Gypsies in the Ottoman Empire: a contribution to the history of the Balkans
Elena Marushiakova and Vesselin Popov (Interface Collection, Volume 22)
ISBN 1-902806-02-6 £11.99
The European part of the Ottoman Empire – the Balkans – has often been called the second motherland of the Gypsies. From this region Gypsies moved westwards taking with them inherited Balkan cultural models and traditions.

Scholarship and the Gypsy struggle: commitment in Romani Studies
Edited by Thomas Acton
ISBN 1-902806-01-8 £17.95
This book marks the development of a new, authoritative academic approach to Romani Studies which locates itself in the problems identified by the Romani people themselves.

Moving On: the Gypsies and Travellers of Britain
Donald Kenrick and Colin Clark
ISBN 0-900458-99-2 £9.99
The only general introduction to the struggle of Gypsies to survive as a people in Britain today.

Smoke in the Lanes
Dominic Reeve
ISBN 1-902806-24-7 £9.99
A classic account of the reality of life as a Gypsy in the fifties when Travellers lived in horse-drawn wagons and stopped by the wayside in quiet country lanes, but were often driven to 'atch' besides main highways as so many of the old stopping-places were fenced off or built upon. This book is full of stories of life on the road and descriptions of colourful characters living for the present despite constant harassment by police and suspicious landowners.

For further details see:

http://www.herts.ac.uk/UHPress/Gypsies.html

Or request a copy of our catalogue from:

University of Hertfordshire Press
Learning and Information Services
University of Hertfordshire
College Lane
Hatfield   Tel: +44 1707-284654
AL10 9AB   Fax: +44 1707-284666
United Kingdom   E-mail: UHPress@herts.ac.uk